Awakening to Inner Creativity

DR. BABATUNDE KOLAWOLE

DEDICATION

To the One who knows.

CONTENTS

FOREWORD

This is the age of knowledge synergy. Far too long in the development of mankind and the application of knowledge content from one field for application and development in others, people have restricted themselves in intellectual straight-jackets, thus limiting the optimization of the results they intend to create. Creativity is an aspect of the breath of life infused into mankind when the Almighty Creator made "man in his own image" (Holy Bible – Gen. 1:27). It is this attribute of making something – an idea, an artifact, a concept, call it whatever name – out of what might or might not have existed before, which is called creativity. Strangely enough, it is engendered out of a certain level of faith in the reality of what is being created, long before its creation. This faith is sustained by fundamental knowledge in the area of creative operation, assurance in the validity of the creative process, trust in the required ability to perform and the essential perseverance in the effort required to follow the dream to its logical conclusion – come what may.

Dr. Babatunde Kolawole must have had a long and insightful meditation on the philosophy of this process and has come to the conclusion that there are essential factors and attributes as well as constraints in the creative equation. He has identified these factors, attributes and constraints. They have been discussed within the context of the subject matter, compiling arguments from various fields of philosophy, religion, science, politics and economics.

For those whose minds might be tied down to a straight-line field of knowledge, this effort might take some digestion, but to the insightful and educated reader, there is sufficient food for thought in *Awakening to Inner Creativity*. For the aspiring artist, scientist, musician, dramatist, inventor, etc, who might be feeling frustrated at the initial stage of endeavours, it is an encouraging must-read.

Dr. Kolawole is a chip off the old block – the Late Professor Joseph Kolawole, his father – was an erudite Applied Mathematician, professional Builder, Educator and Baptist Preacher whom we remember fondly.

This book is recommended to anyone who wants to know what God has created him/her to achieve in life.

Prof. Akin. Akindoyeni, OFR,mni

Abuja Feb. 2014

ACKNOWLEDGMENTS

I would like to thank the Almighty God, through Jesus Christ, for making this dream a reality. Without God, putting this work together would not have been possible.

I would like to thank my dad, Late Prof (Dn) Joseph Ogundiya Kolawole for what he taught me, in the things he said and the things he didn't say.

I would like to thank my mum, Mrs Susan Ayoade Kolawole for believing in me; for seeing greatness in me before I could see it in myself and for helping me build a healthy self-esteem regardless of what the outer circumstances of my life seemed like.

I would like to thank my Fiancée (and hopefully at the point at which you read this, my wife), Iye Danielle Otigba, for believing in me, for supporting me and for letting me know that my dreams can become a reality, for editing this book and for choosing to walk this life's journey with me. I love you.

I would like to thank my siblings – Oluwabukola Olaniyan, Yetunde Kolawole, Oluwabunmi Kolawole and Oloruntobiloba Kolawole for living the essence of this book; for not being afraid to speak and live their truth and for being shining beacons in their various walks of life.

Thank you to Professor Akin Akindoyemi, OFR, mni for writing a beautiful forward to this book. I pray that God will repay you in ways that exceed your imagination. God bless you.

INTRODUCTION

At the age of 22, I wrote my first piece of writing which I titled, "The Living Life" based on the experiences I had at that time. I sent a copy to someone I considered relatively established in writing at the time, to read, review and give comment and he did, returning it with mainly negative views. Since then, I have been reluctant to pen down words from my experiences but as Anais Nin rightly observed, "There comes a time when the pain it takes to remain tight in the bud becomes greater than the pain it takes to blossom." A few years down life's lane, I have not been able to quell this desire to express myself creatively through writing and so this piece is the result of the "pain" that has become greater than what it would have taken to remain silent.

Not unaware that no great work is without its criticism, I have chosen to venture out and yield myself to my life's mission – to be all I am born to be, which includes writing, irrespective of what people think or say and to know, using the words of Dr. Kent Keith, that "in the final analysis, it is between me and God. It was never between me and them anyway."

Though I do not feel qualified to pen down these words, there is Someone who stands beside me and qualifies me, making me worthy of doing so.

I hope that this journey will be for you as exciting and thrilling as it has been for me.

1

GOD DOESN'T MAKE JUNK

E veryone has something to give. Everyone has something special inside. Everyone is innately gifted in some way. This innate creativity is something we all possess but have not all realized yet. The Creative Source* never creates with no purpose in mind.

There is something that you can do uniquely which no other person in the whole world can do quite as well. Once you find this creative outlet which innately resides in you, waiting to be nurtured, you will have no competition; no rival. The root cause of envy is ignorance – the ignorance of not knowing what you truly possess within. You can only be you. If you try to be like anyone else, you limit your potential. Nobody is made quite like you and if you refuse

*Creative Source is the Almighty God, the LORD, the Maker of the Heavens and the Earth.

to nurture this seed within you, it will be lost forever. Your time and energy should be employed in raising your awareness of and focusing on what it is you can do very well, not on what doesn't come naturally to you.

There are approximately seven billion people in the world yet no one has a genetic makeup quite like yours. No one has the same fingerprints as you. There is no coincidence in this. We are all as individual and different as one planet is from another.

While it is absolutely true that the creative seed that lies within you has been gifted to you since birth, it is also true that it lies dormant until certain forces of the mind are activated to bring it to life. I will talk about this at length a little later in this chapter. It is important that you believe that you are worthy of what has been deposited in you. Belief is the cornerstone of all great achievements. A belief in the Divine, a belief in ourselves and a belief in our connection with the Divine are necessary steps to activate this creative seed that lies dormant within. A believing trust in our divinity opens the gateway to the door of creativity.

Our primary purpose and reason for existing is to find and discover who we truly are, to find our real and authentic selves and to fully express this in the best way we can. The most fundamental questions anyone can ask are, "Who am I?" and "What is my reason for existing?" This is what the words inscribed above the entrance of the temple of Apollo at Delphi pointed to. They read "Gnothi Seauton" which means "Know thyself". When you know who you truly are, all other pieces of the puzzle easily fall in place.

Ralph Waldo Emerson said, "The power within man is new in nature and none but him knows what it is he can accomplish nor does he know until he has tried." No one can tell you who you are; you have to find that out for yourself. So when people tell you to be a certain way or do certain things, you must first find out whether what they are telling you to do resonates with you internally or not. Nobody knows what gifts and talents and capacities you possess and you won't know either if you do not take the time to search them out.

The mind has its place in the creative process but many times it becomes an obstruction to finding our creative center because we over-rationalize and over-think things. This is what you hear everywhere you go. Everyone talks about being extremely rational and making sense of every single detail but the Creative Source teaches differently. You can't make sense of the creativity that exists within you. What you should do is trust it. In fact, it is all you can do.

Just like a young eagle learns to spread its wings and believes that it is innately capable of flying just like its mother, we must believe in what we are innately capable of becoming. Take a look at the flow of the universe; look how it bewilders with its simplicity, grandeur and effortless ease of accomplishing. You too can become as naturally divine if you key into the creativity that resides within your heart.

Albert Einstein, the German-born physicist who developed the Theory of Relativity, once said, "I never came upon any of my discoveries through the process of rational thinking." Einstein was connected with something much deeper than the intellect could understand. He knew who he was which is why he was able to manifest what he did in the world. By being true to yourself, you too can manifest your own magnificence in your own unique way.

WE ARE MADE DIFFERENTLY

The uniqueness that you possess is peculiar to you alone. If you would find the route to your heart from which your soul is carved and walk in it, there is nothing you would not be able to accomplish. It is when we deviate and walk the paths of others that life becomes unnecessarily laden with all sorts of difficulties and hardships.

What makes the world peculiar is the uniqueness that each of us possesses. Creativity is the juice of the universe and it flows easily and effortlessly into the world when there are no barricades put on it from being inauthentic.

One of the greatest challenges we have had from time immemorial is that people keep on trying to be what they are not. Until your feet are firmly planted on the path for which your soul is moulded, you cannot manifest true magnificence in this world. You cannot shine in your essence, you can never truly come to know yourself until you are in your creative zone.

THE INACCURACY OF UNIVERSAL ASSESSMENT

There is a one-size-fits-all scale that people have created to assess a person's effectiveness. The problem with this universal scale is that it doesn't work for everyone because everyone is made differently. Everyone will not weigh the same on a universal scale. No one can weigh well on a scale other than the one designed for them.

Unfortunately, this system of universal assessment is still widely practiced and so much creativity is lost because people are not given the conducive atmosphere to express their creative selves. Albert Einstein also said, "Everybody is a genius but if you judge a fish by its ability to climb a tree, it will spend its whole life thinking it is stupid."

God has indeed gifted each one of us uniquely. It is left for us to go on the quest of discovering what our individual talents and gifts are and expressing them in a way that no other person has been able to.

It is not wise to try to blend in with the world simply because you desire to be accepted by others. It is not wise to go against the grain of your heart or to do things simply because they are considered noble or reputable or lucrative. The best thing you can do is what you were created to do. When you do that, all other things fall in place. Only from this place can you find true fulfillment. Anything you try to do outside your authentic lane will leave you with a feeling of emptiness.

That is why so many people after acquiring titles, assets and so many possessions still feel unsatisfied and wonder whether all their toil and labour has been in vain. There is only one thing that can bring you true satisfaction – it is being who you really are. Until you are able to set yourself free, you will not be able to convey your true essence into the world. This will invariably lead to frustration which easily gets transferred to co-workers, families and most disastrously on yourself. Many illnesses stem from people not being true to who they really are.

EXCELLENCE COMES WITH A PRICE

A part of your soul, your essential nature, dies off each day when you ignore the inner guidance that exists within you. Only as you become obedient to the Divine call do you truly become whole.

Many people live lives that are bereft of excellence which is why when you attempt to be different, you are met with opposition and antagonism. People do not like to be reminded of the extent to which they have fallen. They do not want to be reminded of the extent to which they have shortchanged themselves by not living their lives on purpose. They want you to be a part of their mediocrity and will stop at nothing to keep you from moving past where you are.

Acting differently is easy when you are alone. It is when you are in the company of others that acting differently becomes much harder because you have to deal with the criticism that comes with company. Excellence comes with a price. If you want to be truly alive, it is important to live your heart's purpose, not just in solitude but also in society.

"Everyone has creative capacity. The challenge is how to cultivate it", says Sir Ken Robinson. This challenge comes from the pressure that is put on us by the society. Your creative environment must be nursed in yourself first before it can be manifested in the world. When you are whole on the inside, you can then create an outlet for the manifestation of your true self irrespective of the opinions or oppositions of others.

YOUR INTRINSIC VALUE

Everyone is creative. Everyone is born with something exclusive on the inside of them. Everyone has the potential and capacity to make the world a better place. Your intrinsic worth comes by virtue of simply being a human being. It is not determined by what you have or haven't achieved, how smart or dumb people consider you to be, or what you have succeeded or failed to do.

Think of a new ten dollar bill. What is it worth? Ten dollars right? Now think of it all squeezed up and ruffled. Is it still worth ten dollars? Would it not be used to make trade simply because it appears unkempt? Has it lost its value? Of course not. In the same way, this is the way we are as humans. Our intrinsic value is a constant. What happens on the outside may appear to mar what is on the inside, but it does not affect your self-worth.

The reason many people have feelings of inadequacy, worthlessness and low self- esteem is that they have truly forgotten who they really are. They have allowed the world to dictate to them who they are instead of looking inside themselves and remembering who they are. Warren Bennis in his book, *On Becoming A Leader* said, "We like lions and bears instinctively know what to do, but what we know how to do gets covered up by what we are told we should know how to do. Learning then, is simply a matter of remembering what is most important."

Your intrinsic value is in your blood. It's in your DNA. Don't let anyone define who you are, because no one really knows you. You don't even know yourself completely. Only as you begin the journey of knowing yourself do you truly get a glimpse of what the Creative Source has planted in your bosom. This understanding leads to your possessing of your inborn creativity. Without this, your self-esteem is greatly affected, your capacity to carry out worthwhile tasks is greatly diminished and your relationship with yourself and with others is greatly impaired.

YOUR CREATIVE CAPACITY

You have the capacity to create the most exquisite work of art. An exhibition that is unique to just you. You have the capacity to bring into this world something that has not been seen before. You have the capacity to create miracles. Your creativity is part of what makes you human and when you utilize and cultivate it in the way you should, you will be surprised at what is produced through you.

From antiquity, humans have been known to do remarkable things. The ancient story of the Tower of Babel where people's languages had to be confused so that their accomplishing would be limited to the seven wonders of the world will give you a glimpse of what humans are capable of accomplishing when they believe in themselves and work together. Contemplate the Great pyramid of Giza, the Great Wall of China and the Roman Colosseum in Italy. All these are examples of the remarkable creative power humans have when they put it to good use.

You know what's most intriguing about all of this? It's that you have in you exactly what it took to build any of these. The same innate creative genius that existed in them also exists in you. You may not be destined to create another wonder of the world but when you understand who you truly are and live from your authentic place, you will create something wholly new and wonderful, something as delightful as any of the wonders of the world.

Your creative capacity is unlimited but is not automatic. If you don't believe in yourself, you wouldn't be able to accomplish much with what you have been given by God. Henry Ford, the American Industrialist and founder of the Ford Motor company once said, "Whether you think you can, or whether you think you can't, either way you are right."

There is something about the creative power that resides within you. If you accept it for what it is and utilize it in the way you should, you will create and attract for yourself magnificent things. Expect the best of yourself. Accept the best and live your best life. Your expectation is closely linked with your realization.

ARE GOOD GRADES IN SCHOOL EQUIVALENT TO CREATIVITY?

Genius comes in many different shapes and forms. There are those whose gifting comes in the form of intellectual intelligence, who top their class in every subject. But then there are also many other forms of genius which are not any less important for being as yet less celebrated. A person can be an athletic genius, an artistic genius, a musical genius or even an inventive genius.

Unfortunately, because of the way society is built, we tend to focus more on the intellectual geniuses and downplay other geniuses. If a girl doesn't do well in school for example, she is regarded as dull and constantly pressurized by teachers, colleagues and unfortunately sometimes, by her own parents. They don't take time to understand what kind of person they are dealing with or what creative capacity exists in her. They keep on telling her how much harder she needs to work to get good grades without ever deliberately or even passively acknowledging what comes to her naturally.

This is the kind of attitude that kills creativity. If she isn't strong enough on the inside, she begins to believe what she is being told and this belief then becomes a self-fulfilling prophecy. She not only does poorly in her academics, but also begins to do poorly in her area of gifting because no suitable environment was created for her to express herself creatively.

Elizabeth is a great cook but doesn't do very well in school, does this mean she is unintelligent? Chris can dunk a basketball and is the best point guard on his team but has difficulties solving arithmetic sums, does this make him any less valuable or less creative than any of his other colleagues? Martha is a great conversationalist, she makes friends easily and makes people feel at home in her presence but has difficulty understanding history lessons, does this make her dumb? Paul speaks three different languages other than his mother tongue fluently but has not been able to get a B grade in Biology, does this make him less valuable?

Our society is made in such a way that such awesome creative capacities are seldom celebrated. It overlooks how good these people are in their area of gifting simply because they are not as skilled in the things that are conventionally valued as important. And because of the basic human need of wanting to belong, they try hard to work at things they are not gifted at only to end up feeling like failures. People without strong personalities whose gifts lie in areas other than academics have an uphill task of reaching full realization in a world that keeps bombarding them with how intellectual they need to become.

Steve Jobs, Bill Gates and Mark Zuckerberg are school drop-outs because their institutions could not create the enabling environment for them to fully express their creativity. They became so out of touch with an environment that tried to make them conform to what they were not, and so in touch with their true selves that their institutions fell away naturally like garments cast aside. Now the world is better because of these few individuals whose place in the books of history cannot go unnoticed.

Unfortunately however, not everyone is as brave as these. Not everyone has the courage to drown out the voices of society and home in on their own especially when these voices come from their "well meaning" parents, teachers and colleagues.

Practically speaking, the talents and capacities that exist outside the academic world are as needful as those that exist in them. Take for example the fixing of a car. Simply engaging in the theoretical process of becoming a mechanical engineer does not make you capable of performing the work of a mechanical engineer. What you have is potential capacity, not practical capability.

A CHANGE OF MENTALITY

Does this mean doing well in academics is not important? Certainly not! It only means it is not the only important thing. Other areas of creativity exist even if they are not encouraged in many schools across board.

What the world needs is a change of mentality. The world needs to know that everyone is special. Everyone is worthy and everyone is a genius in their own capacity. This should be recognized and encouraged, not cast aside or discouraged in our society today.

I personally salute those parents who are able to see that their children all differ and the one who is intellectual is in no way more valuable than the one who appears not to be. I salute those teachers who are able to assess their students not in the conventional way but in a way that makes each student valued for who they are uniquely. I salute those employers who take time to understand the strengths of their employees and place them in strategic positions so they can fully express themselves. These kinds of parents and teachers and employers are still the exception rather than the rule but with more people beginning to acknowledge and accept the uniqueness and creativity that exists in all, I am hopeful that the current mentality which has swept away creativity in homes, institutions and work places will gradually begin to fade away and a new way of living will begin to emerge in the world.

SCHOOL VS EDUCATION

Mark Twain once said, "I never let my schooling interfere with my education." To be schooled is very different from being educated. A person may not go to school and yet be very educated and a person may be in school for the longest years and yet remain uneducated.

Ideally schooling should incite education but this is not always the case. Most courses taught in schools (especially those in third world countries) are not practically oriented. People are forced to learn what they cannot see or use. It is no wonder many schools are turning out intellectual giants who have no real skill in the real world.

Strictly speaking a person who engages in the real art of a thing is more alive in the moment than one who engages in just the science of it. In the present moment, the practicing person does not defer living but lives fully and wholly. The one who engages in the science of it may have to wait a few years before engaging in practical real-life work. Tests are good but how much do they prepare people for the biggest test which is life itself? Certainly, your ability cannot be determined by some score on an examination sheet.

Let's look at this scenario: Moses finished his undergraduate course in January and because he has not been able to get a job in six months, his parents think they have all the right in the world to be worried, but they never really found out for certain, who Moses really is. The course he studied wasn't even his choice; it was theirs. His parents made him an engineer. In reality, Moses is a passionate artist who comes alive every time he creates a work of art. He has in addition to this passion, a high emotional quotient and so has high-quality, effective relationships with numerous high-profile people.

His parents are unhappy not so much because his staying at home will look bad on his curriculum vitae, but because it will look bad on theirs. They are ashamed to tell their friends that Moses has not yet been able to find a "real" job because somewhere in their own minds, they equate having a "real" job with higher prestige. But Moses' real job is right where he is, right in his home where he makes breathtaking works of art and Moses finds himself torn between living his ideal vocation and being submissive to the loud voices of society. If he is not strong enough, he loses his true zest for living.

John L. Mason rightly noted, "A person is never what he ought to be until he is doing what he ought to be doing." This is tunnel key. Schooling, if done rightly, should lead to practical application - this is education.

The first point of call is the family. Parents are the ones who have the first influence on a child before that child grows older and gets more influence and tutoring from teachers and employers. The best gift parents can give their children is a guided life of their own. Children are indeed one of life's greatest miracles, designed to exhibit their awesome qualities in a unique and astonishing fashion. Despite the fact that they come from you, they are not your own. They were made with their own dreams, goals and desires and though they may share yours, you must never impose yours on them. Instead they should be guided and allowed to grow in an atmosphere of love, grace and beauty so they can learn to flourish and bring out the best in themselves.

HINDRANCES TO AWAKENING TO CREATIVITY

There are many reasons why people don't exhibit their uniqueness and let their creativity blossom. Some of these include the following:

1) **A LACK OF TRUST**: A lot of people simply do not believe in themselves. They do not believe in their inborn capacity to create miracles. They do not believe that they have all it takes to create a unique and blissful life for themselves. The same Creative Source that created the flowers, galaxies, and heavenly bodies also created you. You are made in the image of the Invisible Source and so you have inborn creativity in you. Just in the same way God created things from what was not visible, you can also create from the invisible and make your world beautiful. Without a true belief in yourself, you will not be able to exhibit any of the unique talents and capacities God has deposited within you.

Golda Meir says, "Trust yourself. Create the kind of self that you will be happy to live with all your life. Make the most of yourself by fanning the tiny, inner sparks of possibility into flames of achievement." And Barbara Streisand also quipped, "A human being is only interesting if he is in contact with himself. I learned you have to trust yourself, be what you are, and do what you ought to do the way you should do it. You have to discover you, what you need to do and trust it."

Trust is fundamental and without it, nothing worthwhile can be achieved. You must believe that you truly have something amazing to offer if you are going to offer anything amazing. Envy is simply a lack of belief or distrust in your own God-given capabilities. If you really

15

believe that there is something unique and beautiful that has been placed within you, you will have no reason to envy any other person.

From the same prism, a spectrum of different lights is produced. All lights have their own unique value when looked at from the perspective of the Highest One. When you begin to take the opinions and sentiments of others as gospel truth instead of operating freely from your own creative center, you are shifting from that perspective.

All those who effectively utilize their creative capacities believe in their ability to be creative. This belief spread to their whole being and so their minds looked for ways to be creative, both consciously and subconsciously. Creativity is like a muscle. The more you flex it, the better and stronger it becomes.

A true belief in self completely negates the need for competition. Those who truly believe in their own unique capabilities see that there is no need to compete with anyone because there is nothing to compete for. What competition does a professional golfer have with a professional swimmer? They do not race against each other because their capacities are different. Don't let the veil of envy or jealousy prevent you from expressing who you really are.

2) **THE NEED FOR PERFECTION:** There are many who have not been able to move past a starting point because they wanted everything to be perfect before they began. There is never a perfect time for anything; never a time when everything will be just right. If you wait for the process to be perfect, you will never begin but in beginning, you perfect the process. If you wait to feel ready before

you start, you may never start. In starting, you begin to feel ready.

So if you are thinking of doing anything creative, don't wait for the perfect time because that time will never come. All times are already perfect in themselves. The right time is now. Go ahead and do what you need to do and then you will begin to feel perfect in it.

Certainly, you will make some mistakes, but mistakes on the path to your goal are preparation to guide you toward your aim. They are lessons learned to equip and guide you as you tread along in life. There is nothing that hinders true creativity like the feeling that you have to get it right the first time. You don't. All you need to do is to be your authentic self as you strive towards perfection. The illusion of attaining perfection is what stops the natural flow of creativity from pulsing through you.

Learn from the creative geniuses of the past. Prepare yourself reasonably and then leap. Don't wait for every "i" to be dotted and every "t" to be crossed before you start doing what you should be doing. Dive into the current that propels your passionate desire and swim with your best attitude.

The need for perfection kills creativity. If you want to perform at your peak, remember that the best athletes don't always take the best shots; the best artists don't always produce the best works of art and the best performers don't always make the best performances. What separates creative geniuses from the rest of the pack is their ability to be intensely present at what they do and their ability to direct their attention to what is ahead without allowing what is past affect their present performance. They do not allow the mistakes, disappointments or misadventures of the past stop them from producing the outstanding and incredible results they are capable of.

3) **THE FEAR OF BEING DIFFERENT**: George Bernard Shaw once said, "All great truths begin as blasphemies." People are often averse to what they are not used to. People normally do not crave change even if it is change for the better. They would rather remain in their comfort zone than have their comforts and beliefs challenged or overhauled.

The Pharisees and Sadducees in New Testament literature were threatened by the new teaching Jesus brought which contradicted what they had been taught to believe over so many years.

The creative impulse never shines through a closed heart. It is only when you allow yourself to be open that you are able to see what infinite capacities exist in you. If you go down the lane of great men and women of history, you will discover that many of them were regarded as rebels, misfits and blasphemers. You will also notice that it is precisely because of them that many of the advancements in the world have been made.

You are in great company so don't be afraid to share your heart. Don't be afraid of being different. Don't be afraid of thinking outside the box. Don't be afraid of breaking the rules when required. It is only rules made by God that stand the test of time. Man-made rules are created by men and can be broken by men. The creativity in your heart is meant to be expressed.

4) **THE FEAR OF FAILURE:** There is nothing that paralyses creativity like fear. It saps you of your strength and prevents you from doing anything useful with the creativity that resides within you. If you keep worrying that you are not good enough, you will never be good enough. Your thoughts, beliefs and emotions greatly determine what you are able to produce in the world. Charles Stanley said, "Fear stifles our thinking and actions. It creates indecisiveness that results in stagnation. I have known talented people who procrastinate indefinitely rather than risk failure. Lost opportunities cause erosion of confidence and the downward spiral begins." What Stanley says is true for all aspects of creativity. If you are afraid to launch out because of self doubt or because of what other people may be thinking, you will never be able to create the life you are capable of living. You will never be able to sing the song that is in your heart to sing.

The enemy within is the greater enemy than any enemy without. Self doubt is one of the greatest saboteurs of creativity – that voice in your head that keeps telling you, "You can't do it" or "What makes you think you of all people can do that?" The first step to conquering the world is to first conquer yourself.

Creativity involves a lot of risk-taking. Creativity has a lot of failing factored into it. When you take a risk, the pendulum can swing any way and so many people are afraid of launching out because of what they fear. The most effective cure to fear is immediate action. The more you do (and not just think about doing), the less you fear.

Your fear will not only rob you of your happiness and erode your joy but will also keep you from becoming all you are made to be. One of the greatest discoveries you can make is to find that your fears are not as overwhelming as they seemed to be. One of the greatest discoveries you can make is to become aware that you possess everything it takes to overcome your fear. The longer you think about what you are afraid of, the more it grows. The longer you hide your fear, the stronger it becomes. So instead of cowering in fear, choose to overcome your fear by taking action immediately. It is not by evading but by facing your fears that you conquer them.

Accept no excuses of yourself. Accept no excuse from anyone either. Instead bravely choose to confront your fears with the divine power that resides within you. You gain the strength of every fear you conquer so as you keep facing your fears, you keep growing stronger.

Theodore Roosevelt, the 26th President of the United States of America once said, "Far better it is to dare mighty things, to win glorious triumphs, even though checked by failure than it is to rank with those poor spirits who neither enjoy much nor suffer much because they live in the gray twilight that knows not victory or defeat."

5) **PROCRASTINATION:** Procrastination is a mirage. It is a cloud that never brings rain – a promise that never fulfills. It is the voice in your head that keeps saying, "I can do this some other time", while never allowing this "other time" to become a reality for you. "You cannot build a reputation on what you are going to do," Henry Ford

admonished. Words mean nothing if there is no corresponding action with which to back them up. Words are only a poor substitute for action.

Don't allow yourself to push off till tomorrow what you can do today. The center piece of the puzzle is in God's hands, but there are many pieces of the puzzle that are in your own hands. Use them. Life is unpredictable so do what you can while you can. If a creative thought crosses your mind, do not hesitate to carry it out. Do all you can while you can because you never know how soon it will be too late. Procrastination may seem comfortable but don't let it keep you from taking effective action. Your future may look promising and bright but don't let it stop you from doing all you can now. While you have the advantage, use it to your advantage. Become more than just an empty barrel making an awful lot of noise. Do the things you intend to do.

6) **LACK OF PERSISTENCE:** There is no substitute for the hard work that creativity requires. This is one reason why many people prefer to remain at a mediocre level. When you choose to do the work for which you were created for, a lot of ridiculing and criticism will inevitably follow and if you are not persistent in pursuing your heart-felt desire, your creativity will wither away like a fly that dies within the hour.

Persistence is one of the hallmarks of the truly creative person. Persistent people know that as long as they keep going in the direction of their creativity, there will come a time when the resistance will give way. Calvin Coolidge once said, "Nothing in the world can take the place of persistence. Talent will not; nothing is more common than unsuccessful people with talent. Genius will not; unrewarded genius is almost a verb. Education will not; the world is full of educated derelicts. Persistence and determination alone are omnipotent. The slogan 'press on' has solved and always will solve the problems of the human race."

Nobody ever remembers the names of those who quit. It is those who persisted against all odds that have their names endeared and preserved through history.

2

WE ARE MADE AS SHINING LIGHTS

"Our deepest fear is not that we are inadequate. Our deepest fear is that we are powerful beyond measure. It is our light not our darkness that most frightens us. We ask ourselves, who am I to be brilliant, gorgeous, talented and fabulous? Actually, who are you not to be? You are a child of God. Your playing small does not serve the world. There's nothing enlightened about shrinking so that other people won't feel insecure around you. We were born to manifest the glory of God that is within us. It's not just in some of us; it's in everyone. As we let our own light shine, we unconsciously give other people permission to do the same. As we are liberated from our own fear, our presence liberates others." ~ Marianne Williamson

It has been said that courage is not the absence of fear but the mastery of it. It is not whether we are afraid, but whether we will still go on ahead despite the fear we feel. Any little step forward in the direction of your dream is a step that will be liberating not just to you but to those around you. By simply being yourself, you make other people bold enough to be themselves too. By becoming free, you equip others with their own ability to be free.

The creative seed is embedded in each of us. Unfortunately however, many go to their grave with this seed still unutilized in them. They live mundane lives, not because they feel that is the highest potential for their souls but because they want to fit in with everyone else. By trying to fit in with everyone else, they lose their creative edge and become indistinct not by divine purpose, but by choice.

It's absurd that we try to fit in with everyone else when even in this clique of those we try to fit in with, there will still be those who will not like what we do, no matter what. If everybody will not like you, no matter what, why don't you please God by honoring the divine seed within you instead of trying so hard to please others and blend in with their way of living?

There is a well — an ever-flowing stream of wealth within us and each time we do not honor our own divinity, we deliberately close up our God-given spring and go begging from the urns of others. You are marvelous. You are a glorious being. Once you begin to acknowledge this seed within you, you will be amazed at the quality of life that will be produced through you.

As we face our fears, we discover that what we feared is not so monstrous after all. What really is courage but the ability to be true to ourselves regardless of what we fear?

So many times we overvalue the work of others and undervalue ourselves. We do not believe that we possess within ourselves the same ability that other great men and women possess. We all are able to manifest something unique according to what has been deposited in us. There is greatness within everyone.

In the book of Matthew 9:29, Jesus said "according to your faith it will be done unto you" and so how you feel about yourself manifests into the world, whether you choose to hide by preventing the divine light from shining through you or whether you choose to unapologetically be yourself and let your light shine brightly. The Law of belief, just like the Law of gravity, holds true in a world that is governed by laws.

There is no greater satisfaction than that which comes from knowing that you did the absolute best with what you are capable of doing; that you followed the inner compass that was given to you for guidance and direction.

We all have this inner knowing inside us that we were born not just to exist, but to manifest the divinity within. Of course you can choose not to listen. You can choose to repeatedly ignore the divine call but it won't stop calling out to you. The gifts of God are irrevocable. Your creative seed waits within your bosom like a diamond in a coal mine for the appropriate time when you will deliberately choose to dig deep within yourself and find those treasures that have been available to you all along.

Edward Everett Hale said, "I am only one, but still I am one. I cannot do everything but still I can do something; and because I cannot do everything, I will not refuse to do the something that I can do."

Rules, customs and laws of society which people learn from a very early age suppress their inner guidance system and impair their creative light from shining as brightly as it could. Many times, we brush away what our inner guide says because we look around instead of looking within. We see that if we follow what it says, we will be going against what is normally accepted and so we are quick to conform. We forget that we live in a mad world, a world where many have given up their individuality for a false sense of security that comes with conforming with society; a world where many have not only lost their humanity but their ability to truly live.

So many of the major revolutions in the world were sparked off by those people who decided to free themselves from the shackles of societal thinking and ventured out to do as their hearts inclined. They ventured out to think differently and create their own lane. They followed no hard or fast rules, neither did they let themselves do things simply because others were doing them. They walked boldly to the edge, grew wings and leaped into the vast unknown. Their contribution turned the hands of time and changed the course of history forever.

Indeed many of them were considered mad, yet they did not let what other people think about them change who they really were on the inside. Note, that I am not suggesting civil disobedience, what I am saying is that we should be courageous enough to follow our inner leading even when it leads us away from what is considered normal.

Galileo was thought to be crazy. Emerson's essays were termed 'foolish' by his aunt. Abraham Lincoln was such a positive force for change that he was martyred. These are the ones who dared to be different and to be true to themselves. The world is better today because of them.

It is important that this creative seed within be nurtured and cared for and that if the environment we are in is not suited for it, we create one. It's very easy for the thorns of culture and social patterns to suppress our creative seed so much so that we don't remember we are creative anymore. But our seed never dies. It remains in all kinds of weather, waiting patiently for the right time when we will allow it to spring forth and grow into something amazing; waiting for the time when we will fully express the divinity that we are.

Think about the kind of world that would be created if we all used our creative abilities as was intended for us. Think about a world where people lived true to the one thing that really matters – their true calling and did not squander life by filling it with secondary activities. Think about that kind of world. We would create things of extraordinary magnitude.

CREATIVITY FOR ALL AGES

There are those who read these lines and think that because they have passed what will be termed their "prime", they are incapable of being instruments of creative expression. They say they have passed the age where they can still dare, still believe, still achieve. Regret has filled their hearts and minds and they wish they did something useful with their lives. This truth is for them: The creative flower that blooms even a few minutes before death is still better than that which does not bloom at all.

Nothing is impossible with God (Luke 1:37). Yes, you may have gone down a lane that wasn't yours so far and so long, that you don't have an idea where to start from. But the truth is you can start from where you are, right here, right now. You don't have to cut off completely from your current life as this may spell disaster not just for you but for those around you. All you need to do is to find an outlet for the manifestation of your creative seed and from that tiny outlet, something larger will grow and you will be dazed by the quality of life that will be expressed through you.

It is sad that many people die without truly living. Many die just going through the motions. They die without having ever fed their soul with the creative food it needed. Don't let time, circumstances or other people prevent you from being what you are born to be. No matter how much you have lost in the past, that doesn't count today. What matters is what you are able to do with what time you have left.

I personally believe that we've entered a decade where more and more people are being born with the sole aim of directing others back to the path that has long been forsaken; the path which deep inside we all know to be the true path, but have been too scared to tread all along. Nobody can do what you have been designated to do, so tread your path with pride and take each step with the conviction that each forward movement will light up your soul and keep it glowing.

To spend away existence on trifles instead of true living is the greatest tragedy any human can make of life. We were born not so that we would be led by others who live mundane, inauthentic lives but so we would be led from our hearts to create a life of promise, a life of joy and bliss, a life of heaven on earth.

There is an original power within the well of each one of us which when harnessed, produces something of immeasurable value. The need for authentic creativity is as important as the need for food, clothing or shelter. Just as these things are basic physical necessities of life, your ability to creatively and genuinely express yourself is a basic need of your soul. When you live from the creative place within yourself, you not only enhance your life but you also enhance the lives of all those who come in contact with you. People would go much farther than they are today if everyone lived from the place within themselves that is untouched by the world.

WE ARE ALL CONNECTED

Just as a scorpion sting on the little toe of an individual sends the whole body into a spiral, every individual has an effect on the totality of the Cosmos. We are all energetically connected to one another on a subatomic level. There is no one individual whose state of consciousness does not contribute to the conscious state of the whole world.

We cannot continue to live in lies. No matter how long we have lied in lies, we must now wake up to the truth – the truth that we possess something of immeasurable value within us, the truth that we are all originals and by imitating any other, we devalue our very nature.

Let us therefore harken to the wake-up call and awaken the sleeping giant that lies within. Let us take what rightfully belongs to us. Let us be courageous enough to seek our own treasure and measure our lives not by the standard of the lives of those around us but by the degree to which we are able to open up ourselves to be pure instruments of the Divine Voice.

Our innate inborn creativity is like a dam propped up with supports to keep it from bursting. The supports are the limits we place on our own abilities, our fear to launch out into the beautiful unknown and our ineptitude to believe in how adept we are. Not until we are able to break loose from these supports and remove the shackles that bind us to our fears can we truly know how powerful we are. By being our authentic selves, we get to know what infinite supply of resources we possess, waiting just like a dam to burst open and moisten our dry land again, so it can produce amazing degrees of creative abundance.

THE MAGIC AND THE MYSTERY

Jim Rohn, a personal mentor of mine, and the man who was fondly known as the Great Business Philosopher because of his uncanny ability to blend profound wisdom with creative business ideas once talked about the magic and the mystery of life. He said the magic is that we have so much abundance in and around us; we live in so much richness and we are remarkable beings capable of accomplishing almost anything. The mystery is that not everyone will.

Not everyone will harness and utilize the greatness within. Not everyone will take advantage of the abundance around and inside them. Not everyone will choose to be remarkable.

Human beings have been given freewill; they are able to choose whether or not to fully express themselves creatively or not. They can choose to have lives of mediocrity, lives of 'just getting by' OR they can choose lives of greatness and richness, lives of excellence, lives of becoming all they were made to be. The degree to which we are open is the degree to which the Creative Source will manifest through us. Fear is what keeps us from launching out and expressing who we truly are. The voices of society grow and choke our creativity, preventing its full expression.

Every single moment we live, we have a choice. We can choose now. We can choose tomorrow. We can choose next year. As long as we have life, we have choice. The clause is that we do not know what happens after this very moment. That choice is one that is above the will of every human. Since you do not know what the next moment holds and in this moment, you have been given this privilege, this glorious responsibility, this freedom called choice, why not use it to be all you can be now? Why not be all you were born to be?

DEATH, THE GREAT MOTIVATOR

One of the most efficient means of motivating the self to do what needs to be done is to keep the awareness that you too will die one day and it is only what you fully express that will count in the end. Any deed that is not authentic will not stand the test of time. History only remembers those who against all odds, lived lives of truth and authenticity. No person put this better than William Shakespeare when he said, "Of all the wonders I have yet seen, it amazes me that men should fear knowing that death, a necessary end, will come when it will come." Your life had a beginning and it will have an end. No one will stay here forever. Let us all use what we've been given while we still have the opportunity to.

Let us trust in our connection with divinity; let us accept the truth of how powerful we are, how creative we are, how accomplished we are. Let us take seriously, yet in a playful enjoyable manner, this glorious gift Supreme Intelligence has graciously endowed us with and let us use it to make our lives and the lives of those around us a living heaven.

Let us not disregard the natural impulse of our souls, and be content to live a counterfeit life. Let us not be like the many walking dead – alive but soul-dead. The only difference between their actual date of death and this moment is time.

THE BEAUTY WITHIN

Elizabeth Kübler-Ross said, "People are like stained-glass windows. They sparkle and shine when the sun is out, but when the darkness sets in, their true beauty is revealed only if there is light from within."

Physical beauty is important, but inner beauty is by far, of greater importance. When you are your authentic self, you shine brightly like a diamond because your beauty reflects outwardly what is contained in the inner chambers of your heart. Don't let your light stop shining simply because you have been disappointed or distraught in the past. What makes a diamond a diamond is the pressure it has to withstand to become one. Let your center remain serene like the depths of the ocean and let whatever feeling that may arise be like waves ruffling and tumbling on the surface. Keep your heart in a smiling repose, calm and composed.

I have always loved the writings of the amazing poet, Oriah Mountain Dreamer. Her poem, *The Invitation* is so vital to true living that I think it necessary to add to the richness of this chapter:

It doesn't interest me what you do for a living
I want to know what you ache for,
And if you dare to dream of meeting
Your heart's longing

It doesn't interest me how old you are
I want to know if you will risk looking like a fool
For love, for your dream
For the adventure of being alive...

It doesn't interest me who you are, how you came to be here
I want to know if you will stand
In the center of fire with me
And not shrink back

It doesn't interest me where or what or with whom you have studied,
I want to know what sustains you
From the inside
When all else falls away

I want to know if you can be alone
With yourself,
And if you truly like the company you keep
In the empty moments.

You don't have to ask permission of anyone before you let your light shine brightly. If a different tune is humming in your heart, let it play. Don't refuse your good simply because it has come to you in a different way. The Creative Source is capable of infinite and variable expression and will express through you when you are open.

OVERCOMING CREATIVE INADEQUACY

How do you overcome creative inadequacy and let your light shine brightly? How do you become whole and fully express the divinity within?

Michaelangelo once said, "The greater danger for most of us lies not in setting our aim too high and falling short, but in setting our aim too low, and achieving our mark." Although what Michaelangelo says is true, its opposite is also true. Sometimes we expect so much from ourselves, set the bar so high, that we prime ourselves for failure. Sometimes we are our own worst critics, punishing ourselves for not reaching the moon instead of being grateful that we were able to land among the stars.

So what are some of the ways you can overcome creative inadequacy and let your creative light shine without hindering it?

1) **STEP BACK:** Sometimes, the best thing to do when you feel overwhelmed is to step back. Sometimes you get so engrossed in a thing that you lose the vibe of your creative spirit. It is necessary for you to step back from yourself and from your routine way of being so you can see with renewed insight. Don't let your habitual way of

doing things prevent you from seeing the bigger picture. Remember that you possess unique and beautiful qualities. Remember that you need to replenish yourself so that you do not burn out.

2) **BE IN THE MOMENT:** Your power for creative expression lies in this moment. Your ability to bring your unique flavour into this world lies in the present. There is nothing that kills creativity faster or makes you feel inadequate faster than living in an evaporated state or in a place that is yet to arrive. When you are in the present moment, you are able to function at your brightest and best. You may have to deal with different situations but you don't let any of that bother you. Take back your power by being wholly and completely present in each moment so that you can give from the best that is you.

3) **VIEW MISTAKES IN THE RIGHT PERSPECTIVE:** You don't have to beat up yourself every time you make a mistake. Mistakes are lessons learned. When you make a mistake, do not look long at it. Instead learn from it and let it go. The mistakes you've made simply mean you are human and are not perfect. Refuse to allow the mistakes of the past control your experiences in the present, instead let them be a torch to guide your path as you tread along your creative path. Everything that has occurred or that you have experienced in your life has contributed into making you into the person you are today. Moreover, when you look at events from the Highest Point, you discover that there are no mistakes; only

experiences which are necessary for the developing and evolving of your own soul. Don't let mistakes make you inadequate.

4) **YOU ARE NOT VERY DIFFERENT:** Another thing you should realize is that you are not very different from everyone else in terms of life experiences. Many people, including highly creative people sometimes experience feelings of inadequacy. Everyone has periods when they don't feel absolutely on top of their game. What separates the best people from others is their ability to move past their feelings of inadequacy and still do what needs to be done. Many great works that have been produced have come at a time when everything seemed chaotic. The light within you is independent of the circumstances that surround you.

5) **BE FLEXIBLE:** Learn to be flexible in your approach to things. It is the tree that does not bend when the wind blows that gets broken. Be like water. Be fluid. Take the shape of the container and don't try to fit yourself rigidly into any situation when you can easily adjust yourself. Much of the inadequacy that exists comes from an inability to be able to look at circumstances from different perspectives. Sometimes breaking down the door may not be the most creative option. All that may be needed may just be to find the key and unlock it. Be fixed in your destination to your goal like a star, but be flexible in your approach like a river. There are many roads that lead to the same destination. By allowing yourself to have an open mind, you may just find a more suitable route to accomplish

your desires quicker and easier.

6) **DON'T TAKE ANY KIND OF REPORT PERSONALLY:** The life of every creative person is made up of disappointments, setbacks, criticisms and outright failures but those who are truly creative do not take it personally. They know that setbacks are all part of the process of becoming a better person and so they do not focus all their energies on the negative. Not only are creative people detached from negativity, they are also able to take healthy criticism and are detached from positive reports too. One of the greatest inhibitors of creativity is to reach the point where you think you are making it happen simply because people keep singing your praises.

If you think you are invincible and no longer human, if you allow the applauding to get to your head, you are setting yourself up for a fall. God will not shine through a bloated vessel. So instead of getting puffed up by people's praises, let yourself reach the point where you are not affected by people's reports about you.

7) **TAKE ACTION:** Sometimes, overcoming creative inadequacy requires purposeful action. Over-thinking about a thing can cause you to feel inadequate. After you have prepared yourself reasonably enough, there comes a time when you have to let go of the instruction manual and simply trust. Any kind of action you take at all will give you more confidence to take on bigger ones in the future. There is so much that action teaches that preparation has no clue of. Your self confidence increases by doing, not just by thinking about

doing. As you take the first few steps, your path will be lit as required so you can take subsequent steps. Don't let self-doubt or discouragement from others stop you from taking the relevant action that is needed. William Shakespeare said, "Our doubts are traitors, and make us lose the good we oft might win by fearing to attempt it" and Horace, the ancient Roman Poet admonished, "He who has begun is half done. Dare to be wise; begin!" No amount of preparation alone will win a battle. The battle has to be won by outright confrontation on the battlefield.

8) **CREATE TIME:** There will always be those things that will clamour for your attention but you must learn to create the time you require to creatively express your gift. So many bona fide obligations will crop up during your day and you cannot simply neglect them because you want to be your creative self. What to do is to learn the effective use of your time. Make a list of all the things you will normally do in a day and then ask yourself which ones are of the greater priority so that you can do those first. Your creative work should be high up on the list. There are things you will find that you can do without or do only when you have the time to. These you can without much thought diminish or outrightly eliminate from your schedule. Certainly you cannot control everything that happens in your day. Some unforeseen contingencies will certainly crop up and you need to allow yourself space to accommodate that.

9) **REPLACE SABOTAGING HABITS:** One of the things that easily kills creativity is engaging in a habit that sabotages you. Moderation in everything is a good approach to life. Any habit you perpetually engage in which has the tendency to make you lose your inhibitions is destructive to creativity. When your mind is filled with groveling and debasing thoughts, you are not able to function at your creative peak. Creativity thrives in a loving atmosphere. Anything that takes you away from love takes you away from your innate creativity. A good habit can easily replace one that sabotages you by doing it repeatedly everyday for at least twenty-one days. Life cannot exist in a vacuum and so when you make the decision to stop habits that sabotage you, you must make the decision to replace those habits with something else that supports you or else you end up in a negative cycle of sabotaging habits.

10) **YOU ARE NOT YOUR FAILURES:** There's hardly anyone who set out to do anything worthwhile that did not encounter obstacles or hindrances along the way. In fact, the only people who do not fail at anything are those who say nothing and do nothing which means they are either unborn or dead. Life is like a theatre rehearsal. You keep on practicing till you get it right. It's a good idea to look at all your efforts, not as failures, but as experiences that help you know that you may be needing to adjust what you are currently engaged in or to look to a different path entirely. Failure is not a bad thing, provided you learn the lesson contained in it. Many great people we remember today are people who failed many times before

they attained success. What made them who they were was their ability to learn from their mistakes and keep on keeping on.

HOW TO LET THE LIGHT SHINE THROUGH YOU

1) **BE OPEN:** Creativity is like the wind. You never know where it is going to take you the next minute. Don't let what you did creatively in the past define what your creative steps in the present should be. Be open to fresh inspiration from the Creative Source. Each moment you live is uniquely different from any prior moment and so is the consciousness that is you. Break the chains that bind you to your creative past and be your authentic self now. Be uniquely, abundantly and amazingly alive by living in your most creative place today even if it contradicts all you said and did yesterday. Life is never a constant. The only constant is change. Nothing ever remains the same and neither should you. Let the Creative Grace that wants to flow through you have its way. Allow yourself to be one with the dynamism that flows unencumbered through the Divine presence that resides within you. As you open yourself up to receive, the light of creativity will shine brighter and brighter through you.

2) **ASSESS YOURSELF:** Self assessment is crucial to living a creative life. It is good to periodically examine yourself to see if there are any inauthentic layers that you have unconsciously placed on yourself. Let the light of consciousness shine through every nook and cranny of your personality. Be brutally honest with yourself. The first

step to solving any problem is to realize that it exists in the first place. If you are blind to the parts of your personality that need to be worked on, you will not see a need to improve yourself. As you become authentic, the reflection of your divinity becomes clearer. The Creative Source wants to shine through you but will not be able to do so if you are unwilling. You must remove all the clutter you have put in the way by way of self doubt, disbelief and self sabotage and allow the divine rays to emerge freely through your soul. It is difficult to know who you truly are when there are many rays shining through you. The rays only become unified as you become true to yourself. Only then does your life become a channel for divine creativity to shine unencumbered through.

3) **EMBRACE AND LOVE YOURSELF:** Your battle scars are the evidences of your having truly lived. No ship's purpose is to stay at the harbor though that is the safest place it could be. It is the raging storms that test the skill of the sailor. Never see yourself as unfortunate, instead accept and appreciate all the seasons of your life and embrace them like a mother would her newborn child. Don't deprive yourself of growing by sitting on the sidelines when you should be out in an open confrontation. Let the light of creativity be seen through every part of your personality.

3

EGO: THE INHIBITOR OF CREATIVITY

"Love and ego cannot go together. Knowledge and ego go together perfectly well, but love and ego cannot go together, not at all. They cannot keep company. They are like darkness and light: if light is there, darkness cannot be. Darkness can only be if light is not there." ~ Osho

Our ego is the number one inhibitor of our God-given creativity. Dr. Wayne Dyer defined EGO as "Edging God Out" – a belief that we can take control of our lives without the acknowledgment of the Divine Source working through us. Take love away from God and God becomes nothing because God is love. The whole essence of God is love, nothing more, nothing less. By edging God out, we are choosing to remove ourselves from love.

There is an old saying, "Pride goes before a fall." This is exactly what the ego does to a person. Not only does pride bring about one's downfall, it also clogs the channel of divine creativity. A proud vessel is a full vessel and full vessels cannot be used for divine purposes.

The ego says, "My worth as a person is dependent on the things I have or the caliber of people I know. The more my money, the more my possessions, the greater my self-worth; the more my ranking on Forbes richest list, the greater my worth. The more handsome my husband is, or the more beautiful my wife is, the greater my self-worth." What a grave misconception!

We are not our possessions, neither is our worth determined by the people in our lives. The problem with making possessions or attachment to people a part of ourselves is that if we lose any of these, a part of ourselves gets ripped off in the process. It is important to learn to live independent of things and attachment to people - to truly live a free and creative life.

Don Miguel Ruiz, Jr. who seems destined to walk in the shoes of his father, Don Miguel Ruiz, once said, "There comes a point in life when we grow tired of needing to be right especially when we see how the ego-feeding need affects our relationships with people who just want to be our friends, with the beautiful souls who just wanted to love us. Our attachments don't let us see further than the tip of our own noses... and as we become aware of how our filter of knowledge is constructed, we realize that lasting change only comes from within."

You are not what you do. If you think that your titles or that your social class determines your worth, you are missing the mark. Creativity flows easily and freely when these barricades of ego are put aside. The extent to which we are free from egoistic tendencies is the extent to which divine creativity will flow freely through us.

By clearing the clogs of ego off our creative paths, we make our hearts more translucent and are able to see more clearly. That's what Jalaluddin Rumi meant when he said, "Each of us sees the Unseen in proportion to the clarity of our hearts and that depends on how much we have polished it. Whoever has polished it sees more – more unseen forms become manifest."

HOW EGO BARRICADES CREATIVITY

1) **RELIGION:** The ego barricades creativity when the activities of religion take precedence over the true worship of God. Take for example, prayer. A person can become so vast and skilled in praying that the mode of prayer becomes more important than the sincerity of it. Prayer then becomes a parade and deep down in the heart, the prayer is offered not genuinely but in such a way as to get the attention of other people so as to be looked at as someone who is very "spiritual". The same thing goes for all gifts of teaching, prophesying, leading and singing. When the role itself begins to take precedence over what the role is meant to accomplish, a steep fall is just by the corner. If you reach the point where you begin to say, "I did this on my own", know that you are close to the edge and are about to fall flat on your face. Every little thing we do, no matter how much of our own effort we put in, originates from the Source of all things.

What would your efforts come to if you had no breath? What would it accomplish if you could not freely use your body? What would become of you if your heart stopped beating? Without God working through us, we are nothing and can accomplish nothing. So don't let religious fanaticism blind you from true spirituality. It is possible to be so religious that the true essence of religion is lost. The acts of religion are simply a by-product of true spirituality, an evidence of it. When the acts and not the heart become the centre of the spirit being, then the true connection to the Creative Source is lost and creativity is impaired.

At every stage of our development, the ego lurks. Without careful consideration of our motives and constant self-examination, we are easily deceived to think that we are still open to the Creative Source when in fact we have dampened our own channel by our own hand.

In my opinion, true religion equals spirituality with the emphasis on 'true', however Darren Aronofsky's words tell a relevant distinction: "I think religion is often very different from spirituality. Religion is often about rules and people trying to control our lives who are actually very unspiritual. God can be found anywhere, and in fact, everywhere." Let us take care not to lose the true essence of religion. God leaves the temple when the genuineness of worship dissolves.

2) **REPUTATION:** The best definition I can think of for reputation is other people's thoughts and ideas about us irrespective of whether these are true or not. When you begin to see your

position as something to be grappled for, then it becomes hard to relinquish it when it is time to let go because the position becomes part of your identity. This can lead to all sorts of illnesses and maltreatment of colleagues and friends.

Many celebrities find it hard to contain fame. Their reputation as famous people becomes part of their identity in such a way that if anything should happen to their reputation, they suffer to the same degree that their reputation suffers. Over and over again, we have heard of celebrities who lived such unhappy lives that they were driven to commit suicide. They tried to live their lives compatible with what people thought of them instead of living it compatible with who they really were. They raised the pressure on themselves by trying to fit into the image of the public eye - an image that is as fickle as the blowing of the wind or the color of a chameleon.

Don't get carried away by your religious, social or political position. Positions don't last forever and your status, no matter how long you hold on to it, will eventually fade away. When this happens, what becomes of you? What becomes of the person who was so identified with the position?

Think about what happens to most dictators after they have been forcefully ousted from power. They either get very sick or end up committing suicide. They become incapable of functioning because of the thought that the lost position is who they are. With the position stripped off them, they do not have a clue to who they really are anymore.

Certainly, there is nothing wrong with aspiring to a social, political or religious position. There is nothing wrong with being famous provided you do it without making your position or your fame a part of your identity. These positions are only meant to be used as tools to further a particular purpose or mission and not to change the person you are inside.

You are not your reputation. Your reputation lies in the minds of other people. What you are responsible for is your character. Work on yourself always. Try to be better today than you were yesterday. Race against yourself, not against anyone else. There is a way to be motivated by somebody else's achievement and aspire to reach their level in a spirit of co-operation and not competition. When you work on your character, you create a value that is worth more than gold or diamonds; when you work on your character, you genuinely improve yourself and become an attractive indispensible citizen of society. Whatever you become from that development cannot be taken away from you. It is yours because you earned it and even when people smear your reputation, you have for an assurance a heart that validates you and because this is true, it will set you free.

Winston Churchill said of the truth, "The truth is incontrovertible. Malice may attack it; ignorance may deride it, but in the end, there it is." Let us drop our egoistic tendencies by tending to the one thing that really matters – our character. What other people think of us in none of our business. Rumi said, "No mirror ever became iron again; No bread ever became wheat; No ripened grape ever became sour fruit. Mature yourself and be secure from a change for the worse." When we mature ourselves, we add credit to our real nature while leaving our apparent nature for others to decide as they deem fit.

3) **POSSESSIONS:** One of the most common ways in which ego barricades creativity is through possessions. The ego works through the mind to create an insatiable desire for more irrespective of the need for it. A lot of people are attached to their cars, their houses, their bank accounts such that if anything happens to it, they get overly affected. A person who is deeply attached to a car, for example, may deal a severe blow to someone who put a dent in it, completely out of proportion to the extent of the damage.

There is nothing wrong in desiring money for the good things money can buy. What is dysfunctional is the attachment to the things money buys. There is a wise saying, "Godliness with contentment is great gain." If you want to be happy, it is important to learn contentment. If you want to really enjoy the gifts and bounties of this life, it is important to be satisfied with what you already have. To be content doesn't mean you make no effort to improve the conditions of your life. To be content means you don't get attached to what you make an effort to improve. It is not your possessions that make you rich, it is who you are. A continual insatiable desire for more is an unhealthy desire and this is the cause of many of the world's present problems. There is no end to craving. If you are always trying to grasp things, you lose the natural flow of your life. Only in a contented state can you live a life that is filled with grace, beauty and magnificence.

It is important to hold loosely to the things of this world in such a way that your engagement is only to what is needed and not to what will cause you to become attached. Jesus taught us to be in the world but not of it. It is this same kind of healthy attachment that is needed when a person loses a close election or fails an examination. It is important to know that the election or the examination is not you. It is just something you engaged in and is not synonymous with you. Failing an examination or losing an election doesn't make you any less worthy. Passing an examination or winning an election doesn't make you more worthy.

The degree to which you are free from ego is the degree to which you will easily be able to let go of positions, possessions and people. Sometimes you don't even realize your attachment to a thing until the time comes when you lose it or it is required for you to relinquish it and you find yourself struggling to do so. At other times, it takes a serious illness or near-death experience to bring you back into alignment with your true self so that you can see how ephemeral all things are. Loss of any kind is a great opportunity to know where you stand in relation to things and people. During such times, the ego's grip on you is lessened and the light of divinity has the potential to shine through you.

NO NEED FOR COMPETITION

There is no need to be in competition with any person for anything. It is the ego that always wants to be in competition. You are your own person. You have your own lane. You have been given your own path so tread it with pride, confidence and passion. Your race is not with your peers but with yourself, so focus on doing your best in your own sphere and stop being distracted with what others are doing or achieving. There's no point trying to compete with any other person. When you compare yourself with others, you become distracted and lose your focus. The Apostle Paul said in his letter to the Corinthians (2 Cor 10:12) that those who measure themselves by themselves and compare themselves among themselves are not wise. Accept your own magnificence and individuality and make each moment into something delightful and awe-inspiring.

4) **YOUR PHYSICAL BODY:** Next is the physical body. A lot of people are so attached to the beauty of their physical form as though it were going to last forever. Of course, nothing is wrong with being confident in the gracious body you've been given or the natural beauty you have. What is problematic is when you become obsessed with it and think that there never will come a time when all of it will fade away. Take this truth in: No matter how pretty or handsome you are today, you will lose all of that. Working on your body is important. It is good to love your body and all its parts and be confident in it as long as you are aware of its transient nature and not let it distract you from focusing on what is most important.

Strangely people do not only get attached to a healthy and robust body, but also to a sick body. There are those who derive pleasure in being labeled "an asthmatic" or "a hypertensive" or "a diabetic". They derive pleasure from feeding on the sympathy of others.

The ego says in them, "I am handicapped and so I should be

treated specially." Your body is simply the vessel that contains your spirit. It is an instrument that should be used to further your soul's mission. You are not your body. You are a spirit that has a soul and a body. Dr. Wayne Dyer said, "We are not physical beings having a spiritual experience, we are spiritual beings having a human experience." It is important to know that you are more than just what you see on the outside so you don't get attached in an unhealthy manner. Take care of your body. Protect it. Care for it. Just as you will want to maintain your new car by taking it to be serviced regularly, it is important that you groom and care for your body so it doesn't breakdown before you have completed your mission.

5) **PEOPLE:** Attachment to people. This is one area where it is very difficult not to be attached. Relationships, especially the ones of great value, are responsible for a large chunk of our happiness. It is usually very difficult not to get attached to a sibling or a child or a father or a mother or a spouse. Many people confuse love with attachment but they are not the same thing. Attachment holds on to a person in an unhealthy manner, love lets the person be free. Love cares, attachment needs. If you truly love someone, you should let them be free. Don't hold on to them so tightly that your desire to protect them stifles them or prevents them from fully expressing themselves.

Love is like a plant. Just like a plant blooms with the right mix of sunlight, water and nutrients, love can also grow into something gorgeous and wonderful if you let it be free. When someone loves you not out of compulsion but out of free will, it is a priceless and precious gift. As you live your life as a prime example of love and compassion, others will be drawn to your kind of love. Let love be free and love will freely offer itself to you.

Certainly it is important to protect the people you love from negative influences just like you will protect your cherished plants from the weeds that try to attack your garden. Love but don't become attached in an unhealthy way.

Unhealthy attachment is one of the major causes of protracted or prolonged grieving after a loved one passes on. Of course, there is a place for grieving but when it becomes excessive, it becomes pathological. Reasonable time is enough time to grieve for a loved one as you remind yourself of the fragility of all of life.

DEATH AND THE EGO

Nobody likes to talk about death. Nobody desires it. Many people long for life after death, but nobody wants to die to get there. It is almost a taboo to talk about death yet death is inevitable. It is the ultimate destiny of all mankind.

Should we live in fear of death all the days of our lives or should we learn to embrace it? How can we live fully if we do not lose the fear of death while we still live? Should we not confront it before it inevitably confronts us?

Take time to figure out what is of prime importance in your life and let that be the defining axis on which your life revolves. Ask yourself this question habitually, "Will this matter if I had only 24 hours to live?" What this question does is that it shifts your attention. It shifts your focus. Many things you argue and fuss about fall away in the face of this question. Many things dissolve leaving only what is essential and true to your nature. If you search yourself carefully and you cannot answer "Yes" to this question, then look for ways to diminish or outrightly eliminate those things from your life. If your answer is a resounding "Yes", then look for ways to expand or increase them.

A PERSONAL EXPERIENCE

Many people take no thought about death until someone very close to them dies. Then they are forced to think, study and ponder. I lost my dad on 20th May, 2007 in a tragic and dramatic fashion. The day was Sunday and we went to our local church just like on any other Sunday. Everything was fine, everyone was fine. My dad dropped me off at my place (since I was no longer staying at home but closer to the University for ease of access) and then proceeded home.

I seemed to have sensed that something wasn't quite right but could not put my finger on anything specifically. My flat mate told me I seemed unusually quiet that afternoon but I just shrugged it off and insisted that everything was fine.

It was about 7:30pm in the evening when I got a call saying that my dad had been shot and I should come immediately to the hospital. I dressed up as quickly as I could, not knowing what to expect or even think. Since I was already doing my clinical training at the hospital, I was allowed to walk into the part of the Accident and

Emergency unit that was restricted to other people. As I walked into the resuscitation room, I saw for the first time in my life, the lifeless body of somebody close to me. My dad was lying there, shot and completely breathless. Those who were attempting his resuscitation had given up as it was no longer of any use.

I stood there almost unable to move, my head and heart spinning at the same time. I looked utterly confused. My mum still so ruffled from the incident asked me to tell her what state my Dad was in but I didn't have the slightest clue what to say.

The summary of all this is that it was a very traumatic day for me and one of the most traumatic experiences of my life. The pain I felt during this period, especially the day just before he was to be buried is not one I can put to words. Everything seemed to happen so fast in just the twinkling of an eye.

In that instant, I could see that all his work of striving to see that we, his kids and his lovely wife were adequately cared for was over. In that instant, all he had become, his experiences, his wisdom, was gone. In that instant, his post as a Professor in the university didn't matter. His degrees were not transferrable. In that instant, saying a few last words to him was impossible. In that instant, everything looked so ephemeral and fleeting. Nothing was solid. In that instant, all his future projects and dreams were over. In that instant, all his wealth didn't matter. In that instant my life changed forever.

I learned that life is the greatest and grandest gift of all and all else are just details. I learned that there is a time when it becomes too late to say the words you should have said, to express yourself the way you should have. I learned there is a time when it is too late to do the things you should have done which you just let slip by.

Life flashes back before your eyes like a dream and you wonder how a person so whole and hearty a few hours ago could be so lifeless and cold a few hours later. You see that a couple of seconds is enough time to change a person's life forever. You see how a single moment can be the difference between life and death. You see how death changes everything. You see how it changes your view of the world, how it changes how you interact with other people and how it changes what you consider important. You see how it changes your priorities, your lifestyle and how it changes your personality entirely. The primary purpose of every human being is to fully express the self by grooming one's innate abilities and capacities in each moment. Everything else matters little.

THE FIVE NEEDS OF THE EGO

1) THE NEED TO BE RIGHT

The ego attaches ultimate importance to being right in whatever situation that arises. This is because if the ego is contradicted, it feels as if part of its sense of self is threatened. It feels as though something is about to be taken from it that will threaten its survival. That's why people who commit the most heinous of crimes are able to convince themselves that what they did was for the right reasons and continue to plead their innocence even when an obvious and rightful sentence has been passed in their case.

The ego is so deceptive that if you do not take care to become aware of how it operates in yourself, you may very easily be deceived into thinking that the ego is who you really are. But the ego is not you. Your regenerated being is kind. Your regenerated being is love. Your regenerated being is peaceful. You may think that you have to engage in rivalry or contention just to prove a point or show others why you are right, but in reality, you have nothing to prove. Does the moon try to prove it exists simply because its existence is denied by ten thousand people? Does the sun stop shining and start complaining because a hundred thousand people don't believe in its luminescence?

Simply state your point and leave the rest to be debated by others if they choose. There is nothing to defend, nothing to prove. Accept yourself fully as you give others room to accept themselves fully too. Give up the need to be right and the world will soften itself towards you. Decide to live in your natural state of grace and sacred devotion for all of life. Promote a better world by promoting peace and harmony for all.

2) THE NEED TO FEEL OFFENDED

What makes us react to an offensive statement or comment made by somebody else without thought? It is doubtlessly the ego. Flawless vision is the ability to see 360°. However none of us sees the complete picture, none of us sees all round. We view situations from a particular perspective. Someone else may view this same situation from a different perspective or angle and just because they view it differently from us doesn't mean we are right and they are wrong. It just means that they see differently than we do.

Our capacity to increase our vision in order to accommodate the views of others is crucial to living a life free from the strangles of egoistic domination. To act apart from the ego is to respond when an offensive statement is thrown your way instead of reacting without thought. A response can range from remaining silent and doing nothing while becoming aware of how it feels to have the ego in yourself diminish, to allowing a few seconds to contemplate an appropriate response devoid of offense, one that comes from a plane of a higher vibrational stance than that which you were offered.

Eckhart Tolle said this beautifully when he said, "An offensive comment does not reflect you, it reflects the person making the judgment. The only thing it reflects about you is how you respond to it." By learning how to overcome the ego's need to feel offended, we free ourselves to be all we are born to be. It is in this way that we are able to allow the creative force inbuilt in us to flow freely by being an open expression for it.

Your goal should be to reach the point where you cease to be offended by any statement anyone makes about you. Remember, the world is as it is and will remain so. What you can change is not the world, but yourself. Now, this does not mean that you cannot improve the conditions in the world. It just means that the way and manner in which you do it comes from a change of your internal environment first. If you try to institute an action from a negative state, then you bring about negative energy into the world.

People have a choice to accept or reject whatever advice you choose to offer. Just because they do not accept what you think is best for them, does not mean they reject you. What it means is that they may not know it as best for them yet or what you offer may not be the best for them in that given circumstance. Don't confuse what you advise with who you are. They are not the same thing. People will discard the advice your proffer sometimes and just because they do that doesn't mean they reject you or you should stop giving it. Endeavour to keep your interest in people as you allow them to grow in their own way. Learn to be detached from the outcome of the advice you offer. Respect the rights of others to choose for themselves without making enemies of them.

3) THE NEED TO WIN

Everything in life is not about winning or losing. It's okay to enjoy winning as long as you don't begin to believe that's all there is to living. Losing is an inevitable part of life and there will be times when this will happen to you irrespective of what you do. It does no good trying to keep up the pressure on yourself simply because you want to win everything by all means. Such an attitude is not the attitude of a healthy individual. It can lead to all sorts of ailments and diseases. Allow yourself to go with the natural flow of your life and let things fall in pleasant places for you. I love what Bill Vaughan said, "A few early losses in life relieves you of the pressure of trying to maintain an undefeated season."

Your life has various seasons just like the seasons of spring, winter, summer and fall. You may be on a peak in summer and in a valley in winter, yet all is right and nothing is amiss in the Divine scheme. Times change and seasons change. There comes a time when it becomes imperative to pass the baton to the younger, stronger generation. Don't break yourself up by refusing to be flexible. Allow yourself the flexibility that is required as you feel yourself surrounded by the love and beauty that embodies all of nature.

4) **THE NEED FOR CONTROL OR COMPARISONS**

No, you cannot control everything. Trying to control everything is like trying to make the sun shine at night and the stars glow in the daytime. There are some things that will always be beyond your capacity to control and it is wisdom to accept this. People want to control all events, they want to control all situations and they want to control other people all the time, but this is practically an impossible feat. When things don't go the way you like, as will inevitably happen, the ego becomes bruised and wants to fight back but the fight of the ego is like a man trying to fight with the wind.

The ego also erroneously makes comparisons between people. John is better than Juliet because he is tall and handsome or Mary is better than Michael because she has more influence and more popularity. There is also the ego's need for domination. And this is very rampant in parent-children relationships. I hate to burst your bubble, parents but on the level of the soul, your child may be on the same or an even more evolved level than you are. Yes, you may have more experience than your child, but that doesn't necessarily translate to being wiser. There is so much you can learn from your kids if you choose to be open. It's the ego that closes the mind to the possibility of learning from those much younger than you are.

When you hear a parent argue in the lines of 'It has always been done this way', without any concrete reason to back up what is being said, you know immediately that it is the ego insisting on having its way. Ralph Waldo Emerson once said, "Every man I meet is my superior in some way in that I learn something from him." This should be our attitude to the younger generation. The best gift you can give to your children is your state of consciousness not the numerous words you speak or the force you use to have your way. Children learn more from what they sense than from what is said. Screaming and shouting on children doesn't work because they are watching you and learning from you everyday, not by the words you use, but by the life you live. If you have a higher state of consciousness, your children will naturally absorb this state and become like you. Children are already born wise. If you do something different and say something different to them, they'll pick up on what you do, not on what you say. They will trash your words and key in on your actions. Let your ego take a backstage so that you can have a real and rich relationship with your children.

5) THE NEED FOR SUPERIORITY

You are where you are today because of the mercy and grace of God. So anytime you are tempted to feel or act superior to your fellow man, always remember that. Don't relate harshly with those who are perceived to be of a lower intelligence or emotional state than you are. Remember that they are who they are because of their level of consciousness. If they knew better, they would do better. Hold on to the awareness that if you had the conditions of their birth, their kind of parents, their genetic makeup, their experiences and opportunities, you would act in like manner. Therefore, "Forgive them for they know not what they do." Remember also, that there is nothing that you have which you have not been graciously given by God.

I can hear those who are saying, "But I worked so hard to achieve what I have achieved, to become what I have become. I put all my energy and strength into this" and I say, "This is true. It makes all the sense in the world. You are absolutely right."

However, have you considered this: Would you have been able to accomplish all you did without strength or breath? Did you give yourself these? What would your accomplishing amount to if there were no pulse in your veins? How would you claim a right if your heart did not beat of its own accord? What can you claim as your own if all that is beyond your power is taken away from you?

4

CREATIVITY: THE ROAD LESS TRAVELLED

"Two roads diverged in the wood, and I took the one less travelled by, and that has made all the difference." ~ *Robert Frost.*

The road to creativity is seldom treaded. However, every once in a while, somebody comes along who challenges the status quo and takes action contrary to what the masses are doing. The road to creativity is the road less travelled yet this same road contains an abundance of treasures.

One of the basic needs of humans is the need to belong and this is what the world takes advantage of. Many times, a thing is done not necessarily because it is the right thing to do, but because it is what everybody else is doing. Many times, people sacrifice their own integrity for conformity. People are afraid of what will be said to them, about them or behind them. They are afraid that if they follow the 'unusual' road, they may regret it, they are afraid that since the road is not often travelled, it must be the wrong one, unaware that all these fears are like paper darts that can do them no real harm. Samuel Clemens who wrote under the pen name of Mark Twain once quipped, "Anytime you find yourself on the side of the majority, it is time to pause and reflect."

If you look deeper, you will discover that there is no real reason why you should follow the well-worn path of mediocrity and complacency. The bait of this path is that it seems secure and so people, completely relying on their intellect instead of trusting their hearts, launch out on this road they feel they have control over instead of being open to the Creative Source and letting God work through them in wondrous ways.

By trusting that the divinity that made us is also able to cater, care for and conduct through us, we open ourselves up to a world of possibilities which was previously unavailable to us. Khalil Gibran says, "God has placed in each soul a true guide to the light, but man struggles to find life outside himself, unaware that the life he is seeking is within him."

The creative impulse is the still small voice within that beckons us on, showing us the right way to go. However because it is the unpopular voice in the world, we risk being mocked and teased. We prefer not to risk looking ridiculous in the eyes of others. What should be realized however, is that we will never live our real purpose or be completely alive and fulfilled if we fail to harken to this creative impulse because it is the truth of our being. Because we are made in the image of the Creative Source, every step we take in the direction of truth is rewarded.

We change every single time we honor our creative impulse; we become more ourselves. If this were the only reward this path offered, it would be worth the quest. What is the worth of a life that is lived shabbily in an inauthentic way when it could be lived originally in a genuine way? Again, Rumi said, "Everyone has been made for some particular work, and the desire for that work has been put in every heart." There is an original design we were all engineered with. That original design carries the blueprint for our souls. It carries our soul mission and purpose. However untapped, however unutilized, it is still available to be used by us when we awaken to the truth of who we really are.

The heart is the center of creativity and requires a form of blinding trust. It requires letting go of certainties. It requires a certain degree of letting go of reason, to trust completely. It requires a belief that God is responsible for creating planets and the beating heart, is also responsible for operating miraculously through you when you are open and willing. You don't have to understand every single thing, you simply need to obey.

I like the "leap before you look" expression I once heard which alludes to the path of divine creativity. If you look before you leap, the mind will rationalize, it will give you a thousand and one reasons why taking a leap of faith is a bad idea. It will convince you of the irrationality of your venture and will be sure to let you know that respectable individuals do not do things that are considered strange; that normal individuals are those who are sane and socially obedient, that they follow protocol and breach no rules however contrary to their soul mission those rules may be.

If you leap before you look though, you open yourself up to endless ways in which the Creative Source can work through you and you become a channel for divine expression.

The center of creativity has a divine compass which was made to guide you every step of the way. Like a ship lost in the middle of the Atlantic ocean is guided back on course, the divine compass guides us back to our centre and keeps us from losing our way. This compass is calibrated to perfection. Its origin is the Creative Source so it is able to point in the direction of our purpose no matter how illogical or irrational that may seem to us at the moment.

As we learn to master the art of attaining guidance from this center, we discover that we have all we need for this journey we are made to embark on. By trusting completely, we create the avenue where magic and miracles can happen. The mastery of the creative impulse requires time and continuous practice just as the mastery of any other art.

A little girl may fall off her bike several times but she is not bothered by her temporary failure. She sets herself on her bike one more time because she knows what satisfaction the flawless riding of her bike will bring her. She sees the end and believes that any temporary defeat is worth every bit of it. A young man learning how to drive a car for the first time bashes a gate and feels constantly harassed by other drivers who think his incompetency gets in their way. But he does not give up on his dream of learning because he sees the end. Instead he puts all aside and tries one more time. With constant practice and persistence, he becomes an expert driver and achieves his aim.

Many people set out on the road to creativity, but the slightest hint of a hindrance make them turn back quickly to the common, worn-out road of mediocrity. Don't let this be you. You have persisted in other things of lesser consequence, why shouldn't you persist in what is of greater consequence? Don't let petty obstacles stop you from following what you know in your heart to be true for you. Your heart will always nudge you in the direction of truth and the more you listen and practice, the better experienced you'll get at it. If you keep ignoring your creative impulse, it will fade to the background and your authentic and original life will be lost in a sea of society's mundaneness and mediocrity.

For us to live in the best possible way, it is imperative to live each moment believing and trusting that the Divine Source is able to guide and take good care of us. We need to let go and let God. There are so many gifts waiting to be unwrapped on the path of divine inspiration. For you to receive them, you must be open to receive. This means you shouldn't let your intellect, through rational thinking, barricade your creative channel and prevent you from working in the direction of your high-minded goal or vision. As you take steps of faith, you are propelled in the direction of truth and the senseless begins to make sense.

Deepak Chopra said, "Embrace the unpredictable and the unexpected. It is the path to the infinitely creative within you." If all you ever do is reasonable, then you are living a shallow life bereft of all the infinite possibilities available to you at your beck and call.

To win the best prize, you must risk running through the best route. As you learn to sing the song that was placed in your heart to sing, you become more and more joyful and alive. Ralph Waldo Emerson said, "Let us acquiesce. Let us take our bloated nothingness out of the path of the Divine Circuits. Let us unlearn our wisdom of the world. Let us lie low in the Lord's power, and learn that truth alone makes rich and great."

Certainly no amount of external riches can be compared with the riches and treasures of the heart. God works through you when you let go of your preconceived notions and surrender; when you let yourself be worked through. This is the way of truth.

COURAGE AND CREATIVITY

One of the major reasons why creativity is a road less travelled is because it is not a straight road. Straight roads are easy to travel but "straight roads do not make skillful drivers" as Paulo Coelho rightly observed. Many times, following the pulse of your heart means walking a road that is often lonely and deserted. This makes what you do seem odd and sometimes fills you with doubt. When all the voices are screaming to the left, it takes an enormous amount of courage to listen to the whisper of your heart and move to the right. One good thing about following your own lane is that courage is cumulative. Every courageous act you perform adds to every other courageous act you performed in the past. Soon enough, you begin to exhibit a rare kind of courage you didn't even know you had. Like all great things, great courage develops from smaller acts of courage. Sometimes just remembering how you went on to follow your heart despite all the voices that sang in the opposite direction, helps you live with courage one more time in the present. And indeed, no courageous act ever goes unrewarded.

Friedrich Nietzsche once said, "The individual has always tried to struggle to keep from being overwhelmed by the tribe. If you try it, you will be lonely often, and sometimes frightened. But no price is too high to pay for the privilege of owning yourself." To keep your integrity intact, you must be true to yourself. Indeed, it can be a struggle when you try to live from your authentic place but knowing that nothing else would give you peace, it is not only advisable but necessary that you be true to yourself.

RESPECTING DIFFERENCES

It is important to realize that not everyone thinks the way you do. Not everyone feels the way you do and not everyone will respond to situations the way you do. It is naïve to think that everyone else should be like you. Crucial to getting along with others is the ability to respect each other's differences. We are all created differently and meant to be that way. If everyone were the same, it would be extremely boring to meet myself everywhere. But because of your different upbringing, your different background and your different experiences, I am delighted to meet you provided you are bold enough to express who you truly are, bowing to no one, standing tall and unapologetically expressing your individuality. Unfortunately there is a scarcity of true individual expression in the world today.

Henry David Thoreau (a protégé of Ralph Waldo Emerson) said in his classic essay, *Walden*: "If a man does not keep pace with his companions, perhaps it is because he hears a different drummer. Let him step to the music which he hears, however measured or far away." The creative impulse is vast and inimitable. It sings different tunes to different people. When you are attentive, you will hear the sweet sound of your own unique voice. If you have a little bit of courage, you will manifest things that are unique to you. If you have enough courage, you will manifest things that the world has never been seen before. The Creative Source does not repeat itself in any individual. Our creativity is as unique to us as our fingerprints or the look in our eyes.

If we are able to get to the point where we can openly and individually respect each other's differences, the world will be better for it. A person does not become your enemy simply because the person holds a different belief from yours. In respecting our differences, we grow on the inside and outside both individually and collectively.

Authenticity is recognizable anywhere because we all have a part of it within ourselves, expressed or concealed. If anyone does something that is truly creative, we are able to tell that there is something different about the thing done no matter how dissimilar the thing is from what we do.

WHY IS THE CREATIVE ROAD LESS TRAVELLED?

1) **IT REQUIRES DISCIPLINE:** The road to creativity is the road less travelled because it requires a significant amount of discipline. In treading a known road, it is easy to move forward steadily and swiftly without much thought, but when treading an unknown road, it is important to move forward gently and thoughtfully. This is because the territory is unfamiliar, the route is strange and the way is wholly new. Though taking the road less travelled sometimes yields immediate results, most times the full reward is at the end of the road and it takes discipline to get there.

Many people are discouraged from following their hearts because they think it will be too hard but what they fail to realize is that not following their hearts is an even harder path. Many things that are easy to do, don't have enhanced value, which is why they are easy. They require no discipline of any sort. But indiscipline is very costly in the long run because it sabotages your creativity and erodes the vibrancy of your spirit.

Indeed, the road to creativity is rough and filled with many detours and sharp bends. It requires not just alertness and persistence but also the unique quality of delaying gratification. There is no better way to awaken to inner creativity than by listening to your own heart while drowning out the voices of the masses. It will just take one trial to convince you of the joy and fulfillment that comes from being true to yourself. No matter how unappealing it may seem, see your authentic path through. Don't sell your soul for chaff. Don't be afraid to dance to the tune of your own heart. Don't be afraid to play your own music. We were born, not to be shameless imitators of other people but to be true followers of our own divine path, working with patience, discipline and all things necessary to express ourselves the way we were made to.

2) **IT REQUIRES RESPONSIBILITY:** It is important to realize that your actions have a direct impact not just on you but on a host of others too. When you are true to yourself and accept yourself, you are consciously choosing to graciously shine in your own light and be a shining beacon for others. You cannot allow the weeds to grow in your own garden while you go about tilling the gardens of others. Accepting responsibility for yourself opens your mind, removes blaming and excuse-making and helps your life become more focused and productive.

By accepting responsibility for yourself, you do not accept your success only and deny your failures but you take your life wholly as it is. In this way, you grow, develop and learn from your shortcomings and missteps. Accepting responsibility for yourself is not weakness; it is a mark of true strength. Accepting responsibility can be painful, but once you've accepted it, you discover that, in that moment you transcend the pain of acceptance and your life becomes richer and deeper. When you accept 100% responsibility for yourself, you leave no wriggle room for any kind of excuse and in that way you completely take back your power. In this state, you are able to travel the road less travelled with the confidence and awareness that you are responsible for every decision and choice you make and when something doesn't go right, it is up to *you* to change it.

3) **IT REQUIRES FAITH:** The physical world is real but there is a world more real than the physical – the spiritual world. Most people have their attention completely on the physical. And since their attention is only on the physical, they are unable to focus their hearts on their divine spirit. The spirit is what gives rise to the physical yet in the physical world, the spirit is often undermined.

People that set out to achieve anything of real value, didn't have the slightest idea how they were going to do it, they only had a conviction in their spirits - faith that they were capable of doing what they set out to do, and they accomplished it. Without faith, it is impossible to bring out the best of yourself. Without faith, the creative impulse cannot be transformed into reality.

Many people like to see a thing before they believe it, but the creative path requires that you believe a thing before you see it. Voltaire once said, "Faith consists in believing when it is beyond the power of reason to believe." If you want to be in alignment with your inborn creativity, you must be willing to give up your need to control or understand everything. You must be able to accept that not everything will make sense to you. You must be comfortable with not knowing. And indeed it is faith that will see you through the storms and delays that will inevitably arise on the road to your creative path. Though you do not physically see an end, you see an end through the eye of your heart. This belief is what keeps you keeping on through thick and thin. Mahatma Gandhi said, "If patience is worth anything, it must endure to the end of time. And a living faith will last in the midst of the blackest storm."

4) **IT REQUIRES DEDICATION TO TRUTH:** Another reason why creativity is the road less travelled is because it requires an absolute dedication to truth. Anything that pulls you away from the truth of your being pulls you away from creativity and prevents you from blooming in the best way you can. When operating from your creative center, a brutal honesty is required for yourself. People can feel and sense the degree to which you are authentic or genuine. That's why you sometimes find yourself being drawn to one person and withdrawing from another for no apparent reason other than a strong intuitive feeling that tells you, "It is dangerous to walk this path". When you look back with hindsight, you see that though you were not able to mentally comprehend it at the time, you would have regretted it had you not followed the impulse within your heart. You surely would have landed yourself in a great deal of trouble.

It is very important that you are guided by the truth of your being and that you do not deny what is true for you. Reasoning may be factual but truth comes from the heart and precedes it. Maya Angelou said, "There is a world of difference between truth and facts." As you learn to be guided by the truth of your being and trust in it, you become more authentic. With your newly found authenticity, you are able to travel the road less travelled in better and bolder ways. Your life then expands and becomes fuller and richer.

Sometimes, truth can be difficult to handle, hard to look at and painful to feel yet it is this same truth which when faced, that becomes the gateway for the manifestation of your divine creativity. The primary reason many people refuse to face their truth is because of the pain they are unwilling to encounter.

5) **IT REQUIRES CHANGE:** Growing up as children, it was so much easier when we didn't have to be responsible for ourselves. There was always someone to shoulder our responsibility and it never really mattered how irresponsible we were. A lot of people would like to remain in this state, where there will be no need for change, but this is as unrealistic as expecting a lush garden to grow in the Sahara desert!

Growing up requires change. It requires a reorientation of the mentality and a personal decision to become responsible for yourself. These changes, although ultimately fulfilling, come at a price.

The creative road requires change. The cost of changing is what discourages a lot of people from travelling it. If more effort is required on your part to be your better self, you may think or decide that the additional effort is not necessary and choose to stay where you are. But pain, though unpleasant, is one of the greatest motivators for change. Benjamin Franklin said, and rightly so, that "the things that hurt, instruct". The pain that comes from these necessary changes compel us to reconsider our ideologies and firmly held beliefs and reorient our maps to be able to accommodate the new reality that confronts us. There is nothing constant but change and when you are connected to your creative center, you will notice that change will be required very often. You can be moving in one direction and out of the blue, your creative radar shifts, compelling you to move in a different direction that is uncomfortable or extremely painful especially when the path you travelled previously is one that took so much of your resources and time.

Still, if you do not listen to your creative voice, your soul begins to die. You always have the ability to choose to remain where you are or choose to grow. Change comes with risk and often involves pain but no thing can match the aliveness that comes to your soul when you are properly positioned.

Rebecca Gober summarized the essence of this chapter so beautifully and eloquently in a way not many are able to:

"Here I stand at a Crossroad:
One path, well worn and straight,
The other, leaf- covered
And disappearing, around the bend.
My choice to make –
The safety of the known road
Or the risk
Of the less travelled road…

My mind made up
As I turn to the right
And head down that leafy path
Not sure what lies around the bend
But confident that in risking this unknown
There will be no regret.

No asking, "What if?"
And sometime, years from now,

I'll look back on time
Here, at this crossroad

And I will know —
Taking this unknown road
Led me to know
More of myself."

5

A DELAY IS NOT A DENIAL

"Sweet are the uses of adversity, which ugly and venomous like the toad, yet carries in its head a precious jewel." ~ William Shakespeare

The path of creativity is not a path that is without its thorns and thistles. There are obstacles on this path but these obstacles are not made to be roadblocks but stepping stones for the soul that is determined to live its true purpose.

Indeed, persistence and determination are required to tread this often lonesome path and many times, we may be weary because it seems to us that mountains refuse to move an inch after we have labored a mile. There are no worthy paths that are without their own portion of delay or disappointment but this should, by no means make us give up on our dreams or on our life-given mission. It should rather, be stimulus to spur us on to greater heights of soul maturity.

You see, there is nothing that can be a substitute for your divine purpose. You are either in it or not. This path that you are given to tread is one that is made uniquely for you and you only. If you want your life to be authentic, passionate and alive, it is imperative that you tread this path irrespective of what delays and disappointments you may encounter.

Although this path is strewn with obstacles, it is still the best path for you because no other path can make you feel the joy that this path can. No other path can fill our souls to overflowing like this one can. No other path has the capacity to produce this kind of brimming effect. In reality, it is harder to try to follow a path that isn't yours because it requires you to be somebody else. No amount of drilling in the well of another can make you go as deep as you can in your own.

The Eternal Source is the source of all genius works of art – acknowledged or not. When we act in the interest of our souls, we not only become more ourselves but we dazzle the world as we fill our world with our own blend of uniqueness and creativity.

Ralph Waldo Emerson expresses this beautifully in the following words: "Each man has his own vocation. There is one direction in which all space is open to him. He has faculties silently inviting him thither to endless exertion. He is like a ship in a river; he runs against obstructions on every side but one; on that side all obstruction is taken away, and he sweeps serenely over a deepening channel into an infinite sea."

By the above, Emerson does not mean that there are no "obstructions" on the path of the creative lane, but that on no other path can we draw out so easily a wealth of creative juices; on no other path can we live to be true to ourselves.

"He runs against obstructions on every side but one." What does this mean? It means that all other sides, no matter how seemingly well-fitting cannot create that divine life that is set for us to live.

You function at your best when you live from your creative center. Work then becomes another form of play. It becomes enjoyable because it is the work that was designed for you before the foundation of the world.

Many times, this path is disguised as an obstacle. What looks like a setback is often the very thing that carries your creative spark. No one can deny us walking our path but ourselves. We stop ourselves by ourselves. We see a mild impediment and immediately choose to follow the road of least resistance and then we wonder why we feel such emptiness in our souls; we wonder why we lose our innate aliveness and forget that we have denied ourselves the true expression of ourselves.

Take a cue from ants: as little as they are, when they come across an obstacle, if they cannot pass through, they climb over or they go around. They are always looking for a way. They do not turn back because something obstructs their path instead they keep searching, knowing that their persistence will cause the resistance to give way. They know this secret of nature: Persistence bends almost anything, even nature itself.

H. Jackson Brown said, "In the race between the stream and the mountain, the stream wins not out of strength but out of persistence." It is important that when this still small voice beckons to us, we respond like obedient soldiers undaunted by whatever obstacles may arise.

Let us learn to be the servants of the soul. Let us learn to imbibe this great virtue of geniuses – the virtue of persistence and let us use it to overcome all obstacles in the path of our creative lane.

Aeschylus once quipped, "When a man is willing and eager, the gods join in." By our eagerness and readiness to seek out what is rightfully ours, we evoke in ourselves the power of the Divine to accomplish things through us we would not normally be able to accomplish by ourselves.

The greater the obstacle seems to be, the greater the lurking glory. The Divine is known for wrapping presents in persecution, gifts in gallops and sweetness in seeming sorrow. It is important to keep the awareness that the Supreme Being *always* has our best interest at heart. We "miscreate our own evils" when we do not allow our lives to flow spontaneously and simply; when we decide not to be true to ourselves by following a path that we know in our hearts is not made for us.

One of the most profound statements I have ever heard is one by St. Bernard: "Nothing can work me damage except myself; the harm that I sustain, I carry about with me, and never am a real sufferer but by my own fault." If we could get a grip of the meaning of his statement in the world today, we would be so much closer to world peace than we presently are.

YOUR PATH IS YOURS

No, your parents can't walk your path for you. Your siblings can't walk your path either. Neither can your uncles or your aunties or your cousins or your children. Only you can. Only you are responsible. If you could see all, you would know that there is no situation that was ever designed to cripple or crush you. You will see that Divine Love surrounds you at all times and nothing will be given to you beyond your capacity to bear. You will not be made to wait one minute longer than you can or push one inch farther than you can or rise one foot higher than you can. Only when you are not able to be one with your divine nature do you suffer and this suffering does not come by the fault of another, but by your own fault.

From our birth, we have been bathed in a stream of unconditional Divine love. Our lives were made with the intent for them to function correctly, all our steps guided and all our actions divinely carried out. However, doubt and disbelief cause us to lose this natural protection.

In the light of our new awareness, let us therefore let life flow in the way it was meant to; let us not hesitate to follow the direction the Divine beckons us to; let us have faith that we are equipped with nothing but the best; let us learn to detach from and let go of the things that no longer serve us; let us walk with the awareness that we are made in the image and likeness of the Divine and so are able to accomplish things that will marvel even ourselves.

You can overcome any obstacle and come out clean on the other side because you have within you at all times, the power of the

Divine. This power comes from the Eternal Spring that never runs dry.

Therefore, let us not lose out on real life, walking an illusion because of the fear of what others might think or how they might ridicule us. The time we waste not really living is like a dream and only when we truly chose the life that is made for us do we truly awaken to become all that we are made to be.

Going down the lane of men and women who have accomplished masterfully, who have shown greatness beyond the ordinary, we find that there is a similar thread that runs through the vein of each one of them: They all did not know how they were going to accomplish all they did; they only knew that they were being guided to a life of inspiration and they followed. They did not let pride or arrogance get in the way, and the outcome was a thing of great magnificence because pure, uninhibited creativity flowed through them.

When we leave all we know or think we know behind, we risk all but therein lies the paradox: In risking all, we gain all because we clear our paths for God to work through us. Our miserable interferences only add to the obstacles and make it more difficult to flow in the direction of divine creativity. Always remember that no obstacle that comes your way on the path you have chosen is big enough to contend with the divine power that resides within you. Your obstacles and delays only serve to strengthen you and make you a better person.

THE MAN WHO PUSHED AGAINST THE ROCK

There is a story which was curled from Greek mythology about a man who pushed against a rock. A man was sleeping in the cabin of his room one night when God appeared to him and told him in very clear terms of a mission he had for him to do. He showed him a very large rock that was placed just in front of his cabin and told him that his job was to push against the rock with all his might.

The man did this, day after day, week after week and month after month. He pushed really hard from dusk to dawn using his shoulders to support him. Even when it was cold and windy, he did not give up or give in. Each night, the man came back to his cabin tired, worn-out and wishing he had not met God.

As he began to become discouraged, some thoughts began to crop up in his mind. He began conversing with himself: "You have pushed against this rock for a long time and it hasn't moved. Why kill yourself? It doesn't seem like you are ever going to move it, anyway. Why not just put in your least effort and forget about pushing with all your might?" He began to conclude that he had been given an impossible task by God and that there was no way he was going to succeed at it.

A little while later, he summoned courage and spoke directly to God. He told God, "I have worked hard and tirelessly for you, doing exactly what you told me to do. I put in all my might, my strength and heart yet nothing happened. The rock has not moved one inch. What am I doing wrong? Where am I failing?"

Then God replied: "Son, I gave you a task and asked you to push against the rock with all you've got and you've done just that. Never once did I mention you had to move it. All you needed to do was push. Now you come to me asking, "What are you doing wrong and where have you failed Me?"

"You think you have failed Me? You think because you are exhausted and weary from pushing, you must be doing something wrong? Take a good look at yourself. Look at how your arms and shoulders have developed gracefully, look at the strength now contained in your arms and back from your constant push. Look at your legs, see how your muscles have grown bigger and stronger."

"By obeying My instructions, even though it did not make sense to you. Look how strong you have become through opposition. Look how much skill you have developed. Yes, you truly have not moved the rock an inch, but that was never your task. Your task was to trust Me. Your task was to trust in My infinite wisdom. This you have done without fail. This you have done with persistence. Now you have done your part, let me do Mine. Watch Me move the rock!"

This story I once heard is important because it brings to light the same kind of feelings and reactions humans have when they face delays on the route of their creative path. They begin to think that they must be doing something wrong when in fact everything they are doing may just be right. As long as your heart validates you on your path, don't give in or give up. Don't turn back from the road less travelled simply because you meet a few obstacles on the way. Without these obstacles, you would never truly grow. It is by facing adversity that you grow stronger. Allow yourself to ride on the wave of your deepest and heart-felt path and when a storm comes, know that it is part of your journey and that it brings along with it a lesson of relevance that will inevitably catapult you to a higher level of creativity.

Listen to the timeless words of Emerson in his essay, *Compensation*: "Our strength grows out of weakness. The indignation which arms itself with secret forces does not awaken until we are pricked and stung and sorely assailed. A great man is always willing to be little. Whilst he sits on the cushion of advantages, he goes to sleep. When he is pushed, tormented, defeated, he has a chance to learn something; he has been put on his wits, on his manhood; he has gained facts; learns his ignorance; is cured of the insanity of conceit; has got moderation and real skill."

HOW TO TACKLE DELAYS ON THE CREATIVE PATH

Delays are inevitable and will certainly occur on the creative path as long as you maintain your commitment. Whenever you encounter a delay, remember that it is a sign you are making progress. If you were not in motion, there would be no obstacle to overcome. It is only as you strive to become better that you meet with disappointments and delays.

The following is a 7-step process to tackling delays on the creative path:

1) **ACCEPT IT:** The first step is to accept it and not think of it as something unusual. Delays will occur so let yourself be prepared for

them. Don't deny them. The more you resist them, the harder they become. No one fights with reality and wins. Remember Carl Jung's statement, "What you resist, persists." It is only after you have accepted it that you now have the power to transmute or transform it, and not before. Remember that as long as you are alive and breathing and progressing, you will not get to the place where you will be completely free of delays or disappointments.

Though delays are not what anyone wishes for, they are invariably what make us stronger. Changing seasons give life its deeper meaning. Life would be incomplete without them. Without what we perceive as delays on our creative path, victories would lack their deeper meaning, their true worth, their true significance.

2) **DON'T STAY IN IT:** The second step is not to dwell in it. Delays and disappointments can quickly lead to discouragement which if not tackled can easily lead to depression and sometimes, death. Observe nature; anything that stops growing, immediately begins to die. If it's not remaining green, it begins to turn yellow. A metal not in use begins to rust. Muscles not exercised begin to shrink and when you stop utilizing your potential, it begins to depreciate. The Law of disuse comes to play just like any other law of nature.

Indeed some delays or disappointments may knock you right off course but don't let them keep you down and out. Rest if you need to, then pick yourself up and begin moving again. There is nothing that erodes your potential like stagnation. A stream remains fresh because it is constantly flowing. This drastically contrasts with a lake which is an enclosed body of water with no way to renew itself. It doesn't matter how many delays you meet on the creative path. What matters is whether or not you are willing to get up after every stumble or fall. The one who is not tested every once in a while can never truly know what strength lies in overcoming adversity. Don't let delays and disappointments be your home. Rest if you must, but keep moving on.

Don't engage in self-pity when you encounter obstacles on your creative path. Nothing good comes of that. It only erodes your joy and filches your self-esteem. Remember you are much more than anything that can happen to you. You have what it takes to overcome any delay you face. Choosing to dwell in delay never changes the circumstance. It only saps you of the energy required to overcome it. Delays cannot be avoided, they can only be accepted. So don't pitch your tent in them.

3) **DON'T EXPECT TOO MUCH TOO SOON:** If you tell me you want to build the Great Wall of China, then don't tell me you expect to finish it in three months. If you tell me you want to build the Empire State building in New York, then don't tell me you expect to finish it in a fortnight. If you tell me you want to make a great painting like Picasso's, then don't tell me you expect to complete it within a day. Everything of high quality takes time to create and the greater the value, the more time required to create it. You cannot build a magnificent building without building a solid foundation if you don't want it to come crashing down on you in no time.

Don't be unrealistic. Assess your potential. Assess the place you are, relative to the place you want to be and give room for delays and disappointments that will inevitably arise. Without the turbulence that occurs in mid air and the unpredictability of the weather, the pilot would never become skilled at flying. The journey of a thousand miles begins with a single step and one step is as important as any other step. The tapestry is built by the assembly of many threads. Each thread plays an important role in making the tapestry come to life. Each thread is important. Each thread matters.

So give yourself time. There is no need to rush to the finish line when producing a great work of art. When you expect too much too soon, you create room to be disappointed too much too soon. Don't expect to crawl at birth or begin walking in three months. Be realistic. Don't sabotage yourself. A caterpillar that emerges from its cocoon earlier than it should does not get transformed into the beautiful butterfly that should be the finished product. There is beauty in the cocooning and the time in which it incubates is not wasted time but time required to develop into that beautiful butterfly we all admire and appreciate.

4) **LEARN FROM IT:** Sometimes delays are the result of our own inexperience and ineptitude. Sometimes, we just don't yet know the right combination for opening the creative safe and so we get delayed. One of the best things to do when this happens is to step back and take a good look at the situation again. What this does for you is to help you learn what you didn't know so you can attempt

again with better wisdom and experience.

At other times, delays are entirely due to no fault of ours. Things just happen which are beyond your ability to control and this forces you to slow down or come to a sudden stop. It is at such times you should remember that God will not bring anything your way beyond your capacity to bear. If it shows up in your life, you can handle it. If it causes you to wait, you can walk through it.

Being on the creative path will not exempt you from delays or disappointments. In fact, they will keep happening until you learn what you need to learn to go past that stage in your own evolution. Remember that if you apply yourself, you become wiser from each challenge you face. And you not only become wiser, you gain the strength of each challenge you overcome. The greater the delay, the greater your ability to overcome subsequent challenges. The goal of life is to make you as skilled as you can possibly be. It is your refined skill that enhances your talent and makes you become a better human being, not just for yourself but also for those that surround you.

Whenever you meet with a delay, let your first consolation be that you are making actual progress on the path you have chosen. Delays and disappointments are simply meant to stretch you, not strike you down. Listen to Eliza Tabor: "Disappointment to a noble soul is what cold water is to burning metal; it strengthens, tempers, intensifies, but never destroys it." That's exactly what it is supposed to do. To the soul that is truly alive, delays and disappointments are consumed by the fire that emanates from it. This causes your soul to expand beyond its original limit and so you are able to function at a higher creative level.

5) **DISCIPLINE YOUR DISAPPOINTMENTS:** Just like a rose is not a rose without its thorns, life is incomplete without its delays and disappointments. It is important not to deny or attempt to evade them, but to learn how to tolerate or adapt to them. If you allow your energy to be negative, then a negative state flows into your subsequent actions causing your work to become stale and corrupt. You then end up regretting the actions you take and also begin to reverse the significant steps you've already taken in the past. The pain that comes as a result of such negative actions is far greater than the pain it would have taken to control your emotions and act from a more evolved place. Learn to discipline your disappointments. Always remember that nothing from without can withstand the power you possess within.

The problem many people face when walking the creative path is expecting it to be a smooth ride simply because they are following their hearts. This is a misconception. It is important that just like an athlete prepares herself, you mentally prepare yourself for the hurdles that will come so that when they do come, you will be prepared for them and be better disposed to handle them. When you do not prepare yourself, you are preparing to fail and the obstacles will knock you flat on your face. Preparation is the largest part of learning to discipline your disappointments. When you have prepared yourself reasonably enough, allow yourself to plunge into the current that propels you forward on your creative path so you can deal with every delay with skill and competence.

6) **DON'T GIVE UP:** Nobody is ever remembered for what they attempted. People are only remembered for what they saw through to the very end. It doesn't matter the extent of the delays you encounter, what matters is your ability to keep moving past them. Be patient on the path you have chosen (or more rightly put, the path that chose you). Be persistent, but don't be rigid. Remember that it is the end goal that matters and be cognizant of the options open to you.

If your goal is to climb a mountain, then begin climbing. Keep climbing and if you are met with a delay that seems immovable, don't force your way through. Be open to see if there is an alternative or better way. Make a detour if you have to, but don't shift your focus from your goal of reaching the mountain top. The importance of being flexible on the creative path cannot be overemphasized. Keep a positive attitude and be determined to reach your goal. Be flexible in your approach but fixed on your goal.

7) **BE GRATEFUL:** There is nothing that pushes you past a setback or delay faster than gratitude. Gratitude is one of the best ways of tackling delays. When you are grateful in your setbacks, you are in effect acknowledging that you know that God has prepared the best plan for you and even though you cannot see how, you believe that all is well. This type of gratitude is very powerful because when faced with a delay or disappointment, being grateful is not the most natural thing to do. It is easier, much easier to be grateful when things are

going well for you and no obstacles seem to be placed in your path.

Learning to be grateful in difficult times creates the avenue for you to get out of the rut faster and attracts more things that you can be grateful for. I have devoted a whole chapter in this book to gratitude because of its indubitable importance. Gratitude is tunnel key in awakening to inner creativity.

In times of delay, notice and write down what is going well in your life. What this does is that it shifts your energy and keeps your emotions positive. This then draws more positive things that you can be grateful for. Sarah Ban Breathnach said, "Real life isn't always going to be perfect or go your way, but the recurring acknowledgment of what is working in our lives can help us not only to survive but surmount our difficulties."

There will be times when you feel boxed in and you cannot see any way through. At such times, being thankful is imperative if you are to find a way out. No matter your present predicament, there is always something to be thankful for. In your delay, notice that it could actually have been worse than it actually is and give thanks for that.

Face it, you have been blessed tremendously. You are not presently where you once were. You've not been stagnant since birth. You've made significant strides even if those strides weren't as fast as you expected them to be. Begin by being thankful for what you already have.

TRUSTING THE DIVINE IN DELAYS

"The voyage of the best ship is a zigzag of many tacks", says Emerson. The best men and women aren't men and women who sail smoothly to the top but men and women who constantly face disappointments and delays and still have the courage to keep moving on regardless of how they feel. The best journeys are not only made with tops and crescendos but also with dips and valleys. These delays are like a large crop circle that doesn't make much sense at close range, but when observed from a distance, makes all the sense in the world. We get to see in hindsight, that those setbacks we had were very necessary for us and without them, we wouldn't be where we are today.

Remember that your life's path is not determined by what happens to you, but by how you respond to what happens to you. Your attitude towards any setback directly affects your outcome. How you respond to what happens determines what happens next and what happens afterwards. If you keep a positive attitude regardless of the delays and disappointments, you attract the next positive thing. If you keep a negative attitude about your setbacks, you attract the next negative thing. Some people keep spiraling in a negative circle and blame everyone including the Divine for their present predicament. But not until they have taken full responsibility for themselves can they look outside themselves for a cause.

To break free from a negative circle, you need to take complete responsibility for your life. Blaming anyone or anything doesn't help. It only keeps you stuck there longer. Refrain from ruffling muddy waters. The more you try to control things beyond your control, the less control you actually have. Learn the lessons contained in your delay and move on. God will guide and direct you when you trust completely. Allow yourself to trust in this Infinite Wisdom that grows the flowers and trees.

6

THE HEART: THE CENTER OF CREATIVITY

"You have to learn to follow your heart. You cannot let other people pressure you into being something that you are not. If you want God's favour in your life, you must be the person He made you to be, not the person your boss wants you to be, not even the person your parents or your husband wants you to be. You can't let outside expectations keep you from following your heart." ~ Joel Osteen

The expectations other people have for us are real. Sometimes, they are so real that many don't realize they are capable of living their lives in a different way from what others expect. Joel Osteen, by the above, expresses succinctly the amazing quality of the heart being the center of creativity. The heart indeed is a wonderful gift that God has given us to direct the course of our lives. As with all other arts, learning to listen to your heart takes practice. The more you hear, the more you tend to hear. It is very easy to confuse the voice in your heart with the voices in the world especially when the voices in the world are loud and deafening.

It takes practice, patience and persistence to hear that still small voice within.

Ralph Emerson once said, "Nothing is at last sacred but the integrity of your heart." This means, "Don't sell out. Don't buy chaff for real life. Don't betray your heart." You can fool everybody but you cannot fool your heart. You can rationalize everything with your mind, reason out to baffling degrees, but your heart will not be deceived.

Your heart contains your truth that is why it is unique to just you. No matter how much you try to cover up the truth of your being, somewhere deep down it remains unabashed, unaffected, and uncompromised.

The path of the heart is a golden path. It is golden because it is stuffed with so much valuable treasure. The more you tread, the more you realize the amazing treasures contained in it. The farther you walk in it, the harder it is to retreat. The journey into yourself is the greatest, most exhilarating journey you can ever undertake.

The treasures of the heart are inexhaustible and the creativity that exists in it is unquantifiable. The heart knows a thousand ways to express itself and if that were not enough, it would create ten thousand more. It recreates itself anytime you draw from it. The heart does not capitulate to rules or regulations because it has its own inbuilt compass made to impeccable perfection.

Anytime you lack direction, it is not because the compass is faulty. Anytime you lack direction, it is because you failed to accurately read the compass. When you perfect the navigation of this compass, you can never go wrong.

Lao-Tzu, the Chinese sage made this profound statement: "When the greatness of God is present, action arises from one's own heart. When the greatness of God is absent, action arises from the rules of kindness and justice." And Oliver Wendell Holmes said, "The young man knows the rules, but the old man knows the exceptions." Bear in mind that "young" expressed in the above statement does not refer to biological age but the age of the heart. An old man may be a novice in the art of listening to the heart while a young person may be largely skilled in understanding the wise promptings of the heart.

The greatness of God can only become manifested in your life when you follow the leading of your heart. If you decide to neglect it, you lose touch with your divine nature. It is the emotion of love that the heart responds most to. When you ask the question, "What would love do?" in the quiet of your heart, you prompt the heart to respond. The heart is the center of love and it will always tell you what you need to know if you truly listen.

People can very easily differentiate work that comes from the heart and work that comes from elsewhere because we all have this inbuilt creative compass, such that anytime someone does something from the heart, something within us resonates with the thing done and we know of a truth, that it is coming from that deeper place within – a place we all possess.

WHY PEOPLE DON'T LISTEN

1) **OVERDEPENDENCE ON THE MIND:** One of the greatest reasons why many people do not listen to the voice in their heart is because we have created a society where the vast majority of people depend solely on their intellect for illumination. Many think the heart is weak and sentimental, but is it?

Anyone who has sincerely endeavored to live from the heart is not left without the evidence of its genuineness and originality. The heart sees beyond the mind's reach and feels beyond the body's senses. It is the center of our inborn creativity. This is why the law of the heart is higher than all man-made laws. The law of the heart is God's law.

One of the greatest writers of this age, Paulo Coelho once said, "Insanity is to behave like someone that you are not. The moment you do not fear to share your heart, you become a free person." When we learn to share our hearts with the world, despite the opposing or fearful projections from others, we truly fill our lives and the lives of those around us with magnificence – the magnificence that comes from within.

The mind thinks rationally, but the heart thinks intuitively. There are many situations in which thinking rationally is of proven benefit however the mind is servant to the heart and not the other way round. The heart is the bridge that connects the natural to the supernatural.

What does the mind know? It knows the past and makes deductions of the present and projections of the future based on what happened then. It has no true perspective of the future, nor can it fully comprehend the mystery contained in the present moment. The heart on the other hand, is an intuitive genius that is connected to the Creative Source. It knows the past, is fully aware of the present and can project into the future with impeccable precision. Blaise Pascal clearly understood the ingenuity of this creative center when he said, "The heart has its reasons of which reason knows nothing."

There are many things that will be illogical and irrational with the mind that the heart will be at home with. The heart is like a "faith center" because although you may not know clearly the reason why you are following a certain path, you know it will be alright and in time, you will come to see and understand with your mind, what your heart knew and understood all along. The voice in the head is always very quick to bring to limelight the stark reality of present conditions because it sees only from a very limited perspective – the past.

"Trust the instinct to the end, though you can render no reason. It is vain to hurry it. By trusting it to the end, it shall ripen into truth, and you shall know why you believe", says Emerson in his essay, *Intellect*.

It is very easy to fall into the trap of thinking that the mind through rational thinking alone, can create anything at all. This is true but only to an extent. With the heart as the head coach, you can accomplish so much more than what the mind can even begin to comprehend.

2) **THE ILLUSION OF SECURITY:** Another reason people don't listen to the voice in their hearts is because they crave security. They erroneously think that the past will be like the present and the present like the future when in truth, every moment is alive, different and as fresh as the air we breathe. The mind creates an aura of security but then goes on to sabotage it. It is certainly not wise to base your life only on the things that have occurred in the past.

The heart on the other hand is very flexible. It turns right this week and next week decides to go up. It navigates like a skilled sailor in the midst of a raging storm. Those who have chosen to be led by this amazing center know the thrill and excitement that comes from not knowing what next will happen and this keeps them intensely alive. Rosalia de Castro described perfectly the path of the heart: "I see my path, but I do not know where it leads. Not knowing where I am going is what inspires me to travel it."

The same Creative Source that created worlds also lives in our hearts and that same Power that made the galaxies is also available to us at any moment when we tune into it. What is really unfortunate is not the things we don't have, but the things we do have but refuse to use. So much richness is already gifted to us through this creative center, yet there are those who will go through this life and not even scratch the surface of it.

Henry David Thoreau wrote an essay which he titled, *Civil Disobedience*. This essay was one of the huge motivators for Martin Luther King Jr. during the civil rights movement. In his essay, Thoreau proposes that humans should not be subject to rules and regulations of society, if and when they go against the grain of their inner nature. He advocated swimming with society only when we have that inner acknowledgment and breaking free when we do not.

Thoreau may have been seen as one who advocated rebellion but that was not what he was doing at all. He was advocating for humans to be courageous enough to know that the integrity of the heart is sacrosanct and breaching it is worse than breaching any man-made rule or regulation. The law of the heart is far above any law of the land.

Our present age yields few people who are courageous enough to submit themselves completely to the Divine will. Albert Einstein once said, "I never came upon any of my discoveries through the process of rational thinking." That statement should strike a chord with all those who advocate strongly for the mind. There is a Divine power that flows through an individual when the individual is open. This is the power that flows from the Creative Source into the world.

THE FABLE OF THE MAN WHO DESIRED GOLD

There is a fable of a man who desired so much gold that he left his home, packing his entire luggage with him and travelled far and wide in search of it. After so many years of futile searching, he returned home discouraged and downcast. Laying on the floor helplessly and totally exhausted, his hand hit an unknown lock which opened up into an underground tunnel leading to a place filled with a dozen boxes of pure gold. This fable directly alludes to the creative gift that has been deposited within each one of us. We search desperately for things outside, not realizing that we have on the inside everything we desire.

We've got to be able to reach the place where we absolutely believe our hearts just as we believe that the ground we stand on will hold us. It is important to realize that the One who made the earth, wind and sun is the same One who made this creative center and deposited things of value in it.

We begin to live to our fullest capacity when we begin to trust our hearts in all its capacity. The voice within it is indeed the voice of truth. Let us learn to be obedient heart soldiers and say with Emerson, "Henceforth, I will please God and forever forego the yoke of men's opinions. I will live from within. I will be lighthearted as a bird and live with God." The place of the heart is the seat of God. If your heart is clean, your entire body is clean, but if your heart is defiled, your entire body is also defiled, no matter how good looking you seem on the outside. In the book of Proverbs, King Solomon said, "Keep your heart with all diligence, for from it flow the issues of life."

Your heart is a fertile ground. Whatever you plant is what grows into your life. If you sow evil thoughts, you'll reap a dark life. If you sow noble and graceful thoughts, you'll reap a dignified and abundant life. If you sow creative thoughts, you'll reap a creative life.

When your heart speaks, listen to it. The heart speaks softly and silently yet its echoes are loud enough for those who choose to listen. Don't neglect the impulse of your heart. Don't dismiss it as mere mind interferences. Life can very quickly be covered up by events and activities that can easily drown out the voice in your heart, so choose to safeguard your heart and listen to it. Your heart knows what is good for you. Your heart knows what is safe for you. Your heart knows what is right for you. Your heart knows what is true for you. Listen to other people's words or be moved by their actions and you can be utterly deceived. Look at their gifts and graces, and you can be ultimately misled, but listen to your heart and you will know what is true.

Appearances are not always what they seem. What looks good on the outside may be utterly disgusting on the inside and what appears fragile on the outside may be very valuable on the inside

You only become fulfilled when you live from your heart everyday. Your fulfillment is closely connected with your state of happiness. If you are not fulfilled, you won't be happy. What brings fulfillment has little to do with anything on the external level. More money or a higher paying job will not, by itself, bring you lasting fulfillment. What brings lasting fulfillment is living everyday and every moment from the depths of your soul.

When you are congruent with your innate purpose, you will naturally become happy. When you are congruent with your deepest desires, you naturally satisfy the deep-seated longing of your soul. There is nothing sweeter than the satisfaction of knowing that you are living your life on purpose every moment of everyday. A life of purpose is indeed a life of true bliss.

HOW TO LIVE CREATIVELY FROM YOUR HEART

1) **IDENTIFY YOUR HEART'S PASSION:** You are a natural born genius. Your combination of talents, gifts and capacities exist in you like they do in no other. There is something you can do that no one else can do as well as you. This is because no one else is made quite like you. Find out what makes you come alive. Find out what makes you tick. Find out what makes you reverberate with joy. That's a clue to where your gifting lies. When you are able to identify your heart's passion, you are already well on your way to fulfilling your soul's potential. By building on your gifts, your gifts grow and the world gets served better. By utilizing your natural talents, you expand your capacities and live the life you were made for.

2) **BE COURAGEOUS:** After identifying your heart's passion, you need to be courageous enough to live your heart's purpose. It is one thing to know what you are made for, it is another thing to do what you were made for. Doing what you are made for requires courage because there will be a lot of voices that will attempt to deter you from becoming all you can be. Sometimes, this involves cutting off relationships that no longer serve you or lead to a place you want to go.

It's certainly not an easy thing to stand alone especially when everybody else is doing things that contradict your heart-felt purpose. However, it is important to keep in mind that no degree of disapproval is weighty enough to supersede the disapproval of your own heart. None should prevent you from following your heart's path. In the end, you are the one that will have to live with yourself. Of what use is having the validation of others if you do not have the validation of your own heart?

It is natural to be afraid to step forward for fear of failing but remember that you are never given a path to walk if you are not already equipped with the necessary tools you need to tread it.

The good thing about following your heart's purpose is that once you've done it before, you can easily do it again. Once you've been there before, you will easily go there again. There is enormous power contained in knowing that you have done something before. This knowing forms a significant part of your courage for subsequent endeavours. When you remember what you've done previously, you empower yourself to do more presently. The more things you do with courage, the more courageous you become.

William Cobbett said, "You never know what you can do until you try." And even when you try and fail, you gain profitable experience. Any failing in the direction of your dreams is no failing at all. Indeed, this sentiment was succinctly expressed by the American President, Theodore Roosevelt when he said, "It is not the critic who counts; not the man who points out how the strong man stumbles, or where the doer of deeds could have done better. The credit belongs to the man who is actually in the arena, whose face is marred by dust and sweat and blood; who strives valiantly; who errs, who comes short again and again, because there is no effort without error and shortcoming; but who does actually strive to do the deeds; who knows great enthusiasms, great devotions; who spends himself in a worthy cause; who at the best knows in the end the triumph of high achievement, and who at worst, if he fails, at least fails while daring greatly, so that his place shall never be with those cold and timid souls who neither know victory nor defeat."

3) **ALLOW THE LIGHT OF LOVE IN:** The intelligence of the heart is activated by love. Love is the gateway between the natural and the supernatural. It is love that enables information and ideas to be freely unloaded from the spiritual realm to the physical realm. It is impossible to live creatively from the heart if your heart is devoid of love.

Love is the language that cuts across all creeds, races and tribes. It is the language that crosses all barriers and intersects all hurdles. It is the language that is understood by all who listen to it. There is nothing that can't be done where love is present. Love is the primary cause. Everything else is an offshoot of it. Love is what makes a day come alive. Love is the key. Love is the way. Love is the answer. What makes a day magnificent is when the component of genuine love touches it.

Any work not done in love is as good as work not done at all. Work done in a haphazard indifferent manner brings only partial satisfaction both to the one offering it and to the one to whom it is being offered. For it to be really complete, the component of genuine love must be an undeniable part of it. Do you know that your presence radiates an energy that is felt by all who come in contact with you? Do you know that your energy flows into everything you do?

When your life is filled with love, you become one with all that is divine. When your being resonates in love, you become like God because God is love.

THE HEART: AN INFINITE SOURCE

The heart is a bottomless, endless, infinite source. You can never reach the end of its creativity. The heart recreates itself anytime you tap from it. The more you utilize your creativity, the more you realize you have much more available to use. The opposite is also true. The less you use your creativity, the less creativity is available to you.

It is amazing what we can do when we trust the Divine inspiration that has been given to us and use it by faith. Jesus clearly elucidated this over 2000 years ago when he said, "For to the one who has, more will be given, and he will have an abundance, but from the one who has not, even what he has will be taken away from him." This is true about creativity as it is about any natural talent or gift you possess. The more you harness and utilize your gifts, the more you realize that there is an overwhelming flow of grace in that area in ways that beat your imagination. As your focus remains on your creative center, you will notice that all other things will fall in place.

In Medicine, we say that for you to take care of an ailment, that is, for you to treat a person, you must focus on the cause of the ailment and not the symptoms the person presents with. If your focus is on the symptoms and you keep treating symptoms, you will not be able to get to the underlying cause. But take care of the cause and the symptoms vanish of their own accord. The same is true of the heart. When the heart is right, everything else gets ordered. When the heart is amiss, everything becomes chaotic.

HOW TO ACTIVATE THE HEART'S CREATIVITY

1) **LAUGHTER:** Laughter is the soul's food. Laughter is healing and is good medicine. It costs nothing yet it soothes almost everything. It is has no side effects. The more laughter is contained in your life, the more joy exudes from it.

Laughter opens up your world to new possibilities and insights you were blind to see when it was absent. Laughter fills your world with a fresh sense of vigor and vitality. Nature has a good sense of humour so allow yourself to feel and experience the depth and richness of it. The world and the things contained in it were made for you to enjoy, not endure. Life is meant to complement you, not take from you.

You will notice that the more you fill your life with laughter, the more you are able to feel good about yourself. The more you fill your life with laughter, the more joy you bring to your world and to the world of those around you. Laughter opens up your creative center and enables you to be so much more creative. It is one of the key ways of activating the creativity that resides in the heart. Take Og Mandino's timeless advice: "Laugh at yourself and at life. Not in the spirit of derision or whining self-pity, but as a remedy, a miracle drug, that will ease your pain, cure your depression, and help you to put in perspective that seemingly terrible defeat. Never take yourself too seriously."

2) **GRATITUDE:** Gratitude is the second way to activate the heart's creative center. As long as you are alive, there is always something that you can be grateful for. The thing about gratitude is that it works in the same way the other laws of the universe work. The more genuine gratitude you hold in your heart, the more you will enable things to come your way for which you can be grateful; the less genuine gratitude you hold in your heart, the less you will be given to be grateful for. So instead of looking at what you do not have, be grateful for what you do have.

Remember that what you have was once among the things you hoped for, and in that state, so much more will come your way for you to be grateful. There is a lot around you right now that you can be thankful for. Don't get so caught up in the hustle and bustle of daily living that you forget what is most important- that you forget that life is the grandest gift and the rest are details.

Each day, each hour, each moment, there is a genuine reason to be thankful and if you will take time to count your blessings, you will see that you have been given so much already. As you count your blessings, you activate a torrential deluge of abundance.

3) **MEDITATE:** If you are constantly surrounded by noise and activity, you will not be able to connect easily with your creative

center. There is nothing wrong with having a lot of activity going on around you provided that you also have times when you can be silent and be all by yourself. Meditation is so central to activating the heart's creative potential that without it, you will certainly be lost in secondary activities that don't mean much.

When you meditate, you connect effortlessly with your creative center and become aligned with God. Many of the world's greatest inventions didn't come from continual mental activity but from a place of inner stillness and poise. Taking a casual walk in nature is an excellent way to meditate. A few deep and conscious breaths can also help you feel more alive and keep you grounded. You can also sit in silence as you focus on the attributes of the Supreme Being who is infinite, boundless and ever-creating.

Rollo May said, "In order to be open to creativity, one must have the capacity for constructive use of solitude. One must overcome the fear of being alone."

No posture is an absolute requirement for meditation. As long as you are able to create an internal atmosphere of stillness, your posture doesn't matter. It is not enough that your external environment be still, the stillness has to come from within you too. The most advanced forms of meditation involve maintaining a peaceful and still spirit in the midst of a busy and ruffling day. Meditation is the key to serenity.

James Allen, in his timeless classic, *As a Man Thinketh* said, "Who does not love a tranquil heart, a sweet tempered, balanced life? It does not matter whether it rains or shines, or what changes come to those possessing these blessings, for they are always sweet, serene and calm. That exquisite poise of character which we call serenity is the last lesson of culture; it is the flowering of life, the fruitage of the soul."

4) **HEALTHY RELATIONSHIPS:** Your associations matter. The people you habitually surround yourself with greatly influence who you are and what you become. If you associate more with those who live from within and listen to their hearts, you will begin to think and act like them. We are vibrational beings and so it is not possible to associate with a person without part of the person's personality rubbing off on you in some way.

Never think you are under any obligation to associate with anyone. Choose your associates very carefully. Unapologetically separate yourself from anyone or anything that causes you harm or lowers your vibration. Associate with those who will build you up and inspire you to be all you can be, not those who will pull you down or deter you from becoming all you are able to become. Make no one into an enemy but be sure to choose your friends wisely. Be strong enough to protect your territory and your heart because "out of it flow the issues of life." The role of your associations in activating your creativity cannot be overemphasized.

You can only rise as high as the people you surround yourself with. Remember this anytime you want to choose an associate.

5) **GOOD SLEEP:** The fifth way to activate your creative genius is

to get good and regular sleep. Sleep is a form of meditation. Having adequate sleep is crucial to enhanced creativity. When you are asleep, your subconscious mind takes over. When you are asleep, you are completely resigned in the arms of God freely, completely and wholly. From this place, you can wake and be privy to an amazing level of creativity that the world has not yet been privileged to see. In your subconscious state, you connect with the Divine in a way that your conscious mind seldom can.

As a result of the constant mind activity associated with wakefulness, it is difficult to be in a state that unifies you wholly with the Divine. This state is easily accessed by the subconscious mind. If you don't get enough sleep, you will not be able to wake up renewed and refreshed to take on more creative tasks. Sleeping sharpens creativity. The Irish Proverb which says, "A good laugh and a long sleep are the best cures in the doctor's book" certainly has a lot of truth to it.

Sometimes in the middle of a creative block, taking a nap can be the best block breaker. You sleep over it and then find yourself waking up to an intense clarity knowing exactly what you need to do. Sleep indeed is a nourisher of the soul and an activator of the creative spark within.

HARNESSING THE HEART'S CREATIVITY

When creativity calls, drop everything else and follow unquestionably. Your life absolutely depends on it. When you have a sudden perception or a creative spark, it is unwise to leave the thought alone and tell yourself you will come back to it at some other time. The time to start is when the thought is new, when the emotion is at its peak. The time to start is when the feeling is at its highest.

This is the time you can easily channel creativity and make it work for you. Creativity is like a flicker in the dark. If you do not capture it when it flickers, you lose the thought forever. If you decide to postpone it, you lose the emotion contained in it which is an absolutely necessary component of what makes your creativity attractive. So harness your powerful creative spark and let the passion that is contained in your soul freely flow into your purpose.

"The inner fire is the most important thing mankind possesses", says Edith Södergran. Don't allow that fire to cool off instead harness it and keep it flaming hot so that you can easily transfer this energy to those who come in contact with you.

IGNITING CREATIVITY IN CHILDREN

Little children are some of the best creators ever because they have not yet learned to fear. They are carefree, innocent and easy going. They are not afraid to make mistakes, and are ever willing to rise up anytime they fall. They are naturally inquisitive and always ready to explore new ground. There is a lot we can learn about creativity from little children. There is a lot we can learn about harnessing this amazing gift that lies in silent repose within each one of us.

If we will not educate fears and uncertainty into our children, they will grow up truly believing in their inborn creativity and will not be afraid to think and act in brilliant and creative ways. Little children are like wet cement; while they are still very young, they can be moulded, their creativity can be ignited and a fire that is lit then, can last a lifetime.

If your children see creativity in you, they will easily harness it. Children are very good learners. They learn more from what they sense than from what they are shown and more from what they are shown than from what they are told.

7

LIVING IN THE MOMENT

"Do the duty that lies nearest thee, thy next duty will move closer and then become clearer." ~ Goethe

The unpredictability and uncertainty of the creative path is the reason why so few ever travel it. Living in the moment is one of the sure ways to awaken to inner creativity. The untrained mind thinks to a time when life will be full of everything, when everything will be perfect, oblivious to the fact that all future moments begin in this one. How can the perfect future exist if this moment is not made perfect by our actions? How can we get to 'that point' in the future, if we are not doing something today, no matter how small, that inches us closer to a better tomorrow - the tomorrow of our dreams? I will attempt to answer these and other questions in the course of this chapter.

The past and the future are reference points. They only exist in thought. The only true moment is now. Yesterday is in the past, tomorrow is a dream but today is the day you can be all you were born to be. Today is the day you can begin writing those lyrics. Today is the day you can begin singing that song. Today is the day you can begin writing that book. Today is the day you can begin nursing that child. It is in this moment that your power lies, not in the past or the future.

LIFE ON PURPOSE

Many times, we think we are not living on purpose, we think to a time in the future when we will be this or that, we think to a time when we will fully become ourselves. But how can we fully become ourselves in some future moment if we are not fully ourselves in this present moment?

Our primary purpose in life is to be able to live life in this moment so fully and truly that we are naturally propelled to greater heights in the future. It is in honoring this moment that the future becomes beautiful. The future is nothing more than a bundle of numerous moments.

Whatever we aspire to become or think to achieve is in reality only a thought in the head. That is your secondary purpose. So when I hear people say, "I am so scared I am not living my purpose", I wonder what they are talking about. What they are actually doing is worrying about a point in the future (which may never come) and in that state of worry, they miss the miracle contained in this moment, they miss the sheer joy and mystery of it. It is important to be present in this moment so that we can be fully alive and let creativity flow through us. It is futile to dwell in the past or think excessively about the future.

THE POWER IN THE PAST

The past is a good reference point to this moment. It gives the advantage of experience and helps us to be able to alter our lives in better ways in this moment. Aside from this, the past has no useful purpose and dwelling in it is what is truly meant by not living one's purpose. It is what truly impedes divine creativity.

Walter Malone said, "Wail not for precious chances passed away! Weep not for golden ages on the wane! Each night, I burn the records of the day, at sunshine, every soul is born anew." and Ralph Waldo Emerson added, "Finish each day and be done with it. You have done what you could. Some blunders and absurdities no doubt crept in: forget them as soon as you can. Tomorrow is a new day: begin it well and serenely and with too high a spirit to be encumbered with your old nonsense."

To wail over chances missed, or opportunities passed is to waste real life. This is a sure way to barricade your God-given creativity. Let the past only serve as a reference and a lesson so you can live a better life right now and walk a different path beginning today. We all have done things in the past we are not particularly proud of or may even be ashamed of, but the past is the past. Tell yourself, "What is past is past. I refuse to lose real life dwelling in an evaporated state. The only time I have is now and I will be useful in it."

THE GLORY OF THE PAST

The creative impulse is not only hindered by the hurts and mistakes of the past, it is also hindered by the glory of it. We bask in a state of euphoria from past experiences and dwell there instead of utilizing all the opportunities God has given us today. This way, we impede the divine impulse and cause ourselves to function in ways far less than our normal creative capacity. Escaping to the past feels like a more pleasant reality than this present moment. This manner of escapism makes our lives very inauthentic.

Always remember that this moment is as it is because in the Divine scheme of things, no other moment could have been better placed than this. What is happening is happening as it is destined to in the grand design engineered before the world began.

Let us therefore learn to live true lives, let us not live in our thoughts, but embrace this present moment no matter how unappealing it may seem. For anytime we dwell in a lost state, whether pleasant or painful, we lose parts of ourselves that cannot be recalled again.

ON REGRET AND RESENTMENT

Regret for aspects of our past can serve a useful purpose if it causes us to improve the state of our present affairs. However, if it causes us to have feelings of self-pity or unworthiness, then not only does it serve no useful purpose, it also hurts the joy of the moment.

Resentment has no useful purpose. It does not hurt the other person. It hurts you. If you really love yourself, you would let resentment go so you can be a happier person. Resentment is very different from anger in that it is not usually verbalized or vocalized but always internalized which makes it all the more destructive. It is capable of causing deep emotional, psychological and physical damage to the person who holds on to it.

Many times, resentment stems from the belief that people should act in a certain way towards you. And when the person doesn't, as is often the case, we grow resentful. What we fail to realize is that it is not possible to change people. People can only change themselves. Don Miguel Ruiz has important advice when it comes to dealing with resentment: "Accept others the way they are. You cannot change other people. To try to change them to fit what you want them to be is like trying to change a dog into a cat, or a cat into a horse. They are what they are; you are what you are." Trying to make other people fit into our own mould is not only a very unrealistic way of living but also a very negative way of living.

The importance of having boundaries cannot be overemphasized. If people continually malign and mistreat you, maybe you should consider whether these are the people you want to have around you. We all make mistakes and nobody is perfect. When someone makes a mistake that affects us, true repentance means apologizing for the wrong suffered but also making a decision to walk a new path. If someone just apologizes but then goes right on to do the same thing that caused the mistreatment, then that is not a true repentance. It is only a ploy to keep you in their negative sphere and we should be wise enough to recognize it and bold enough to dissociate from it.

Look at all the uprisings that have recently arisen in the world. They arose as a result of dictators trying to make other people to be what they wanted them to be. The uprisings in Syria and Turkey are good examples. It is obvious that forceful coercion does not work. Leadership works best by influence, not force.

It is also important to note that resentment also blocks the gateway by which the Divine can communicate through you. Resentment attaches you emotionally to the person you resent, and until you break loose from the chains that hold you to that person through forgiveness, you cannot truly be free.

A lot of times, those people we resent don't even have a clue they did anything wrong. A few times they do, but that doesn't change anything. Our resentment is not their problem; it's ours. We are the ones who have to deal with it, not the other person. Someone once said, "Resentment is like drinking poison and expecting the other person to die."

HOW TO RELEASE THE PAST

How do we release resentment and regret? How do we break free from the strongholds that bind us to another person in an unhealthy manner? How do we stop the negativity of the past from affecting the vibrancy of this present moment?

The simple and most immediate answer is forgiveness; Forgiveness of ourselves and forgiveness of others. I will deal extensively on the issue of forgiveness in a subsequent chapter so I will only say a few words here.

Mark Twain once said, "Forgiveness is the fragrance the violet sheds on the heel that crushed it." This is an excellent definition of forgiveness. Hermann Hesse, the Nobel Laureate and German Poet made a very important observation when he said, "If you hate a person, you hate something in him that is part of yourself. What isn't part of ourselves doesn't disturb us." If we took an honest evaluation of ourselves, we would see that Hesse's statement is very true. This internalized anger becomes an open door way to plainly hate another person.

There is a Zen proverb that says, "Let go or be dragged." This is as true of forgiveness as it is of all other areas in life. If we keep holding on to the hurt or shame or pain, we would never truly be free to be the creative people we were made to be.

One of the biggest steps in letting go of regret and resentment is realizing that no one else can make you feel the way you do. No one can control your feeling for you. If it seems like someone else is controlling your feeling, it is because you have given them your power – the power that is yours to keep, not give away.

Have you noticed that sometimes when two different individuals are exposed to the same set of circumstances, one goes away extremely resentful or angry and the other goes away completely unaffected? What do you think is the difference between these two individuals? The difference is perception. It is in the way they each choose to view their situation. If somebody else can respond in a different way to the same set of circumstances that sends you into a spiral, then how can the circumstance or situation be your problem?

The real problem is your perception. If you can alter the way you view the circumstance, then you can alter your feeling and invariably alter your state of consciousness.

Byron Katie came up with a series of questions called "The Work" that helps people look inward instead of outward. It asks four (4) personal questions when dealing with regret or resentment.

1) Is it true?
2) Can I absolutely know that it is true?
3) How do I feel when I believe that thought?
4) Who would I be without that thought? and a "turnaround" of the four questions.

The turnaround projects the spotlight not on the person you have a grudge against, but on yourself. It helps you see that in the moment you judge someone else's actions as resentful, you are acting in a resentful manner towards that person.

ON THE FUTURE

Creativity can also be impeded by dwelling too much in a futuristic state. Not that there shouldn't be planning, or preparation. Not that there shouldn't be intention or walking in the direction of your planned goal, but being so much in a future state that one misses the presence in the irreplaceable today is a sure barricade to awakening to inner creativity.

The Creative Source works through us when we are open and

when we allow the day unfold in the way it is designed to and are present in it, not absent in the past or pulled by the future.

WORRY: THE INHIBITOR OF CREATIVITY

What causes us to be uneasy? What causes us to worry? What causes us to have stress, anxiety and tension in our lives? Is it not thinking about the future or the past in an unhealthy way in the present?

When you rehearse a mental future or a mental past out of fear, the fear causes you to be uneasy, to become worried, to be anxious and stress-filled. This comes from a failure to realize that God is all in all, makes all and works through all that are yielded and open.

When you worry, you invariably bring about a state of uneasiness and anxiety in yourself. Aside from anticipating events in the future with fear, worry makes you think about events that occurred in the past with regret which impedes the present moment. You cannot live efficiently if you allow worry to control your thinking. You cannot live effectively if you are not fully present. Allow yourself to trust completely. Allow yourself to enjoy each moment as it comes. Feel safe in the knowledge that the Creative Source that is responsible for your beating heart and the rotation of the planets is also responsible for supplying you with the strength and grace you need in each moment.

Accept that there are things that will always be beyond your control. Focus instead on the things you can change. By trusting completely, you eliminate worry and create the avenue to function at your very best.

There is absolutely nothing good that comes from worrying. Not only does it steal your joy, it also drains you of the strength you need to function at your very best in this moment. Worry is a kind of unbelief because what it infers is that the Creative Being is not trustworthy enough to take care of your trivial needs. If worry could accomplish anything good, it would have several millennia ago but till now, worry has not been able to accomplish any useful purpose.

So the next time you are tempted to worry, switch your mind over to the awesomeness and simplicity of creation. What in this moment can you be grateful for? Focus on it and let yourself feel the beauty and goodness that is characteristic of all the wonders of creation.

"Learn to enjoy every minute of your life. Be happy now. Don't wait for something outside of yourself to make you happy in the future." Earl Nightingale admonishes.

Do not dream of touching the moon when you have failed to acknowledge the beautiful flowers at your feet today. Do not dream of a state of bliss in the future when you have failed to realize all that is beautiful and blissful around you today. We must begin looking at today with different eyes. We must begin looking at today in a different light. Today is an irreplaceable gift and we should take it for the present that it is. Each day brings a new gift. Let us unwrap our gifts and be grateful for them.

Robert Kiyosaki, the multimillionaire advised, "Take time to appreciate your present condition, it will only become a memory tomorrow." And Babatunde Olatunji observed, "Yesterday is history. Tomorrow is a mystery. But today, today is a gift that is why we call it the PRESENT."

Let us measure each day not by what we get from it, but by what we contribute to it. What God-given talents have you unwrapped to be of benefit to yourself and others today? How have you allowed the Creative Source work through you today?

All future states are simply thoughts in the head. All future events are owned by the Creative Source and He does with it what He pleases. We can plan all we want, dream all we want, project all we want, but we will never know what tomorrow may bring. Tomorrow, or even closer, the very next moment can be so radically different from the last that we may be left all but nonplussed.

If then, we have no control over the circumstances of the future, let us utilize the only moment we have, which is right now, to its fullest capacity. Robert Ingersoll said, "This, in my judgment is the highest philosophy: First, do not regret having lost yesterday; second, do not fear that you will lose tomorrow; third enjoy today."

GOALS AND THE PRESENT MOMENT

Q. Does being in the present moment mean we should say "yes" to everything and have no goals?

A. I have been asked this question a couple of times, so I figured out it was important enough to bear repeating in this book. This is the conversation that ensued between me and JT (name altered for privacy reasons)

JT: Does being in the present moment mean we should act as a doormat?

ME: It does not mean that we are to act as a doormat. It does not mean that we should consent to any and everything that comes our way in the present moment. What it means is that in living in the present, we are open to God and our spontaneous actions are always inspired by God. It means that in this state, we have the ability to say, "Yes", "Wait" or "No". God always provides the right answer at the right moment when we are open and trust completely.

JT: Does this mean that we should not have goals or aspirations or dreams?

ME: Not at all. It's okay to have goals, aspirations or dreams. These only become flawed when we let them fill our minds completely in such a way that they usurp the beauty of the moment. While we live in this human form, we cannot do without planning or dreaming or setting goals. So it's a matter of what we let take the foreground in the present moment. We do not deny what could be accomplished in the future, but we also do not use this moment as a means to an end to accomplish what could be done in the future.

I use the word "could" deliberately because though we like to think we have total control over things and over our own lives, we really do not. We only have control to the extent that the Creative

Source has given us permission.

Now, there is a present way of planning or dreaming. You can be so consumed by the future that it draws away your life force from the present moment and takes away your power, or you can be present as you take steps to accomplish what it is you aspire to achieve.

Take for example, writing a book. In my mind, I have this goal to write a book. So I take a pen and a paper and write down what I would like to accomplish. Let's say I decide to write three pages everyday for an hour to enable me reach my goal. All through the time of writing, I am actively living in the present moment. I am not drawn to the end of the book or wanting to reach the end faster than it should come. I am simply enjoying each moment of each hour as I pen down the words that ultimately become the book that achieves my goal.

In my writing, I am present. In my thoughts, I am present. In my concentration, I am present. And in this state of mindfulness, I am able to harness fully the power of the Divine and allow it to flow through me as I write. I write the book in the present, take it to the publisher in the present and release it to the public in the present.

I have goals, but I live in the present as I achieve those goals and my life is filled with all the grace and beauty that is embodied in all of nature.

Watch a flower or a tree or a blade of grass - watch their gracious growth, watch their gracious becoming. They are never striving to become taller than they already are, but are content with whatever height they are in the moment. In their contentment, they grow to marvelous heights and become graciously adorned. Everything in God's creation is an example of present moment living.

LIVING EXTRAORDINARILY

How can we have extraordinary lives? How can we do things that will marvel and dazzle the world? How can we do what nobody else has done before? How can we bring a unique variety to life? It is by allowing ourselves to be led by the Creative Source in the present. It is by allowing ourselves to become conduits in this moment for divine creativity to flow through us. A word of encouragement, an affirmative look, or a simple smile can be all somebody needs to get through their day. Be open, allow yourself to be an outlet of divine manifestation. Let everywhere you go be as bright as the spirit within you. Carry your own weather.

FREE YOUR MIND

The natural untrained mind has a particular momentum for thinking. It keeps on having an inner dialogue which, by itself, will keep you from being present in the moment. You are most alive when you are aware, not when you are thinking. Awareness and thinking are not the same thing, even though thinking could occur when you are aware.

Let's use the internet for an illustration. When you begin browsing for the first time, you get carried away by all the advertisements and placements. You are drawn to almost anything you see. Later on however, as you gain experience, you begin to notice that it is not everything that calls for your attention you subserve. Human thoughts run like the internet. As you increase your awareness, you learn not to believe everything you think. Thoughts still cross your mind, but you learn not to pay attention to them and in so doing, you gradually diminish their hold on you.

Thoughts are like clouds. Your awareness is like the sky. If you leave the clouds alone, in time, your sky will become clear again. However if you let yourself be carried away by each cloud that crosses your horizon, you easily lose touch of the sky. You lose your oneness with life. Your mind becomes dense and you are not able to be a vessel for the manifestation of Divine creativity.

When you take thoughts for what they are, momentary objects floating in space constantly in dynamic motion, you then become more alive and present. This, I think, is what Bob Marley meant when he said, "Emancipate yourselves from mental slavery, none but ourselves can free our minds."

Now there are those who are thinking this guy must be crazy. Is he saying we should not think at all? What will become of us if we are no longer able to think? What other life will we have? No, that's certainly not what I am saying. What I mean is this: When you are in the present moment, you are easily able to think more clearly when thinking is required, because your thoughts become more focused and direct. This does not mean that thinking becomes unnecessary. It just means that your thoughts no longer control your awareness anymore. You are not carried away by the continuous clatter of thoughts that is characteristic of many people's entire existence. Only then can you see a flower and really appreciate it or eat the heart of a watermelon and really enjoy it. You become aware of the futility of engaging the mind in anything it suggests, and in that way your mind becomes the servant and your spirit, the master. Your thinking becomes divinely and creatively inspired. What you think, say and do has the unmistakable stamp of the divine embossed on it.

If you take a survey of all those who inspired and brought about lasting change in the world, you will notice that all of them lived an intensely present life. Some of them didn't live long (as assessed by human standards) but their impact and contribution lives on decades after their demise. Examples abound: Martin Luther King Jr, Mahatma Gandhi and Abraham Lincoln. Their lives were all marked by the simplicity that is characteristic of moment-by-moment living. It is not difficult to see why they accomplished much in the world.

Affirm this as often as you can: "Today, I shall force nothing. My life shall be like nature, taking its normal course, just like the rising of the sun or the gradual blooming of a beautiful flower. By letting all, I shall accomplish all because of the greater Power that resides within me."

Q. Does the present moment equate with anything that goes on in the present?

A. The present moment does not equate with the things that go on in the present moment. Driving a car, or talking to a friend or reading for an exam are examples of things that go on in the present moment but it does not equate with the present moment itself.

The present moment is the awareness that is always present in the background of whatever activity you engage in. If you let yourself be consumed by what happens in the present moment, you are no different from those who are consumed by incessant thoughts in their heads or carried away by events of the past or future. If you lose your present moment awareness, you lose your connection with the Creative Source and impede your natural, spontaneous inborn creativity. Only in remaining aware, do you retain your innate power.

Don't let your mind deceive you into thinking that there must be something wrong with this moment the way it is. No, this moment is perfect just the way it is. Your real life is determined not by the things you think should have happened or not happened to you, but by how intensely alive you are in this moment. Your real life is determined by the degree to which you realize the fleeting nature of all things and how you conduct your life in that realization.

BRING YOURSELF BACK TO THE PRESENT MOMENT

Many times, because of how the world operates, even the best of us sometimes get lost in activities that we engage in. At such times, it is necessary to be realigned with the present. Some of the ways in which we can do this are:

1) **THE CONSCIOUS BREATH:** Breathe. As simple as this is, many people forget to breathe. Remember this by taking a few

conscious breaths now and then in the middle of your busy schedules. Inhale deeply and exhale slowly.

When you breathe consciously, you are deliberately breathing in the life force God gave you and reinvigorating your cells in the process. I am sure you have noticed that when people are in a negative state, like anger for example, they tend to breathe shallow because in that moment, they have disconnected themselves from the Divine.

It's okay to get angry once in a while, but if your life is constantly characterized by anger, or any other negative emotion, you begin to gradually poison your cells and shorten your lifespan. It is important to harness positive emotions like love, gratitude and peace while minimizing or eliminating negative emotions like hate, ingratitude and anger. Positive emotions open you up and make you more receptive to freely take in the life force contained freely in nature.

One way you can do this is to take early morning walks when the town has not yet become very active and when the air is fresh and unpolluted. That's a really good time to reinvigorate your cells.

There are other times during the day when you can feel the wind kiss your face like the kiss of a woman's lover. This is a good time to open yourself up, and take in conscious breaths. Don't let yourself get so busy with activities that the simple act of breathing consciously few times everyday gets lost. Allow yourself to breathe freely and consciously. Take in at least 2-3 conscious breaths everyday. The more conscious breaths you take, the better you feel and the more creative you become.

2) **MEDITATE:** There are various ways to meditate. Even the conscious breath is a form of meditation. To meditate simply means to still the mind, so that you are clearly congruent with the Divine.

Some people engage in spiritual exercises depending on what kind of religion they practice. Others meditate by sitting still and listening to the silence within. Some have quiet times just before the day breaks, where they are easily able to connect with the deepest part of themselves. Essentially, any type of meditative practice engaged in is much better than none.

Meditation stills the mind and reduces the intensity of thoughts that constantly race in its arena. It anchors you with the divinity within. Make meditative practice a regular part of your daily life and you will begin to function in better and more efficient ways.

3) **KEEP REMINDERS:** We are creatures of habit. Once we begin to engage in any kind of activity over prolonged periods of time, we easily get lost doing it. A married woman with kids in kindergarten, building a career and supporting her husband can get so consumed by her daily activities that she forgets to take time out for herself. If she keeps this habit long enough, she then becomes disconnected with her Source and is not able to give the best of herself anymore.

It is wise to have daily, weekly and even monthly reminders that remind you of the person you are on the inside. Just like taking a morning bath is refreshing, engaging in activities that keep you in touch with the person you are on the inside is also refreshing.

Many books may not teach you anything new, but they have the capacity to remind you of those things you already know but may have forgotten. This is also very important. Remind yourself by attending seminars, conferences and presentations that center around spirituality. Be a regular member of your place of worship so you can be frequently reminded of the values that should be held dear and guarded jealously in your heart. The more reminders you have, the more centered you become in the present moment.

4) **EMBODY THE BEAUTY OF NATURE:** There is a divine stamp on everything that is natural. Being aware of anything natural keeps you centered in the present moment. Notice the stars. Notice the rainbow. Notice the clouds. Emerson once said, "The sky is the daily bread of the eyes."

When you notice and put your attention on anything that is natural, you immediately pull your attention away from the mind which is where it gets lost most of the time. Don't let yourself become so used to nature that everything in it simply becomes a routine. Nature is always new. The moon you see today is not the same as the moon you saw yesterday. No matter how many times you look at the sky, you cannot capture the same view twice. You are just like nature. You are not the same person you were yesterday and you will not be the same person tomorrow, you are today. You cannot touch the same moment twice because each moment carries with it its own uniqueness and grace.

You change with every breath you take. As long as you are open, a marvelous transformation can take place within you at any time. The only thing constant is change so let yourself notice the changes that occur in nature and also in yourself. Allow yourself to remember and appreciate all the goodness and beauty that surrounds you each day. Accept the uniqueness of each moment and let yourself be guided to a better place by the Infinite Wisdom that guides all of life. Your goal should be to get to the point where living in the present moment becomes your natural state.

It is important that you allow yourself to be completely acquiesced to whatever the present moment holds and not allow yourself to be distracted by past thoughts or drawn into the future before it arrives. It is important to remain mindful in your day-to-day interactions.

Have you ever chattered a cab for fifteen minutes on an unfamiliar route and half way through your journey, you notice that you don't even remember what happened during the last few minutes? You don't remember what turns were made, what kind of trees you passed along the way or what caliber of people crossed your path. If you were asked to tread that same route again all by yourself, you find you are unable to do so simply because you were occupied in your thoughts all through and failed to notice what was clearly obvious. This certainly is not the way to live.

There are many advantages that come with living each moment in a present way. Some of them are enumerated below.

THE ADVANTAGES OF LIVING IN THE MOMENT

1) **IT IMPROVES YOUR HEALTH**: When you are present and honoring the moment, your health improves dramatically. This is because you don't get worked up about the future and so you don't increase the stress hormones in your body. You don't get burdened by the past either and so you don't function below your optimum level or capacity.

In a mindful state, your chances of being depressed are drastically reduced and your immune cells are boosted making you less susceptible to opportunistic diseases. Dr. Bruce Lipton, author of *Biology of Belief* once said, "One of the most important discoveries any human can make is to discover that our own brains are our best pharmacies." This is very true. We begin to notice it for ourselves when we train our minds to stay focused in the present.

The University of Oxford's Center for Suicide Research, found that depression can be reduced through changing brain activity by up to 50% with mindfulness meditation. The Bible is a book I know from experience can help with this. When you meditate on the promises of God in it, you find that you are healthier and feel more vibrant to face the day.

2) **IMPROVES YOUR RELATIONSHIPS:** When you are living in the moment, you have a heightened sense of awareness and alertness. Your relationships become so much more meaningful and profound. The depth of your relationships is always enhanced by

your ability to focus on what you are doing in the present. People can intuitively know whether you are really listening to them or not, even when your gaze is fixed on them in a listening pose. It is something that can be sensed. That's why many will prefer to be around those kinds of people who will make them feel good not only by what they say, but also by what they do not say. That is, by the way they listen without judgment, not just with their ears, but with every fiber of their being.

There is a category of people who are repulsive by the kind of vibration they emit. You just notice that in their presence, you feel way off. You may not be able to place your hands on anything specifically but you know that something is just not right with them and if you try to go on with the relationship, you find that you end up regretting your action.

It may be that they have a spirit that is racy and not yet at rest. By their agitation and association, they infect you with their vibration and the longer you stay in their energy field, the worse off you become. Protect your energy by staying off these kinds of people. Don't even apologize for it. It is your birthright!

3) **ENHANCES YOUR MEMORY AND FOCUS:** When you are present, you are not only able to remember things more clearly, but you are also able to focus more clearly. That's why professional athletes like Michael Jordan, Kobe Bryant and Lebron James make it a point of duty to engage in some form of meditative practice to keep them centered and help them improve their game by enhancing their

ability to focus. With increased attention and concentration, there is an increased level of performance.

It is the same with remembering. When your mind is not perpetually on the pedal of the past or in a flight to the future, you are able to remember more powerfully because anytime you are required to recall anything from the past, you remember that you were intensely present at those moments and so it is so much easier to recall. You find that you are easily able to remember intricate details.

Indeed the power of the present moment cannot be overemphasized. If you want to produce any kind of professional work, you require a certain amount of focus and true focus requires that you be well grounded in the present moment.

4) **KEEPS YOU CONNECTED TO THE CREATIVE SOURCE:** It is only when you are living in the present moment that you are congruent with your divine impulse. It is only as you keep being present that you remain a channel for creative expression.

What you can assess from a mindful state is far greater than anything you can assess from living in the past or living in the future. Oliver Wendell Holmes rightly said, "What lies behind us and what lies before us are only tiny matters compared with what lies within us." When you live apart from the present moment, you severe your connection with the Creative Source and stop yourself from living an authentic and genuine life.

The core of our true nature, the authentic part of ourselves is always meant to be in alignment with our divinity. We are the image of the Invisible Source. We become one with God when we are true to ourselves and to our God-given nature. Only when we are connected to God can we share all that we are with others in a spirit of grace and gratitude.

Let us therefore, let the love that flows from the Divine inundate our souls and flow effortlessly into our lives and the lives of those around us. Let all who come in contact with us know without an iota of doubt that we are truly connected to God.

8

GRATITUDE

"Gratitude unlocks the fullness of life. It turns what we have into enough and more. It turns denial into acceptance, chaos into order, confusion into clarity. It can turn a meal into a feast, a house into a home, a stranger into a friend. Gratitude makes sense of our past, brings peace for today, and creates a vision for tomorrow." ~ Melody Beattie.

A day without gratitude is like a day without air. Gratitude is so important to daily living that its opposite can darken a day and make it gloomy. It is as easy to be grateful as it is to be ungrateful.

A glass that is half-filled with water can be viewed in two ways: half-full or half-empty.

There are many people who see their lives as half-empty glasses. They do not look at what is full in their lives, they do not see the things the Divine has already graciously provided them with, they do not sense the grace that exudes from their personality every moment. They focus on what they don't have, they focus on what is missing in their lives and so they attract more of what is missing. Then they wonder why their world is as gloomy as it is. They do not see that they are the ones who all by themselves staunched their own channel by their own hand.

Then, there are those who look at their lives as half-filled glasses. These are those who are consciously aware of the abundance that already exists in their lives. They see God already supplying their needs and are confident much more will be done for them. They are aware that just being alive is a privilege and they remain grateful for every stride they take, every moment they live, and every breath they take. Their lives are an embodiment of gratitude and by law (The Law of Attraction), they attract more of what they can be grateful for.

It's so easy to forget or ignore the numerous blessings that fill our lives for which we should be grateful. Some we consider insignificant, others we become so accustomed to, we take for granted. What we don't remember is that no form, no matter how solid it seems now, is ever going to last forever. It is the destiny of every human and everything that is man-made to dissolve. A noble man of old, Job once said at a point when he was severely afflicted, "We bring nothing at birth; we take nothing at death. God alone gives."

There is really nothing that you have that you have not been given. No person exists in your world that has not been brought in by the mercies of the Creative Source. Unfortunately, it sometimes takes losing something or someone that is very dear to us for us to realize the immense gratitude we owe to the Creator for the people in our lives and everything we temporarily possess. Nothing is meant to be taken for granted. Everything commands our gratitude in some way.

No two moments in life are the same. In essence, everything is in motion. When we learn to be grateful for the tiniest, minutest details of our lives, we attract bigger things for which we can be even more grateful. It is essential to learn to see the blessings the Creator has endowed you with, with new eyes – eyes that see through the familiar and do not neglect the trivial.

To open your eyes to a new day, to rise up from bed at dawn, to eat, to walk, to see, to undertake successfully daily activities with appreciation is to live in a place of gratitude and awe for all of life.

There are indeed many people around us who are unable to do these basic things and would be overwhelmed with joy and immense gratitude if they could only have for a day, the lives we've been given. Perhaps, these people are lessons for us to see that no matter what challenges we may be going through, there is always someone somewhere who wishes they could have what we take for granted today.

CAMOUFLAGED BLESSINGS

Camouflaged blessings are those blessings which seem negative because they disrupt our already well-planned schedules, yet in actual fact, carry with them untold treasures that will make our lives so much more fruitful and useful.

Many times, however, we are so fixed in our ways, so set, that we fail to see what we should be grateful for in the things that look like distracters; in those things that take us off our already well-planned route. The phrase, "Man proposes, God disposes" bears repeating everyday of our lives so we can keep the awareness that life is beyond our will in every moment.

The essence of this phrase is this: We make plans, but it is the counsel of the Divine Will alone that will stand. King Solomon said it this way in the book of Proverbs: "A man's mind plans his way as he journeys through life, But the LORD directs his steps and establishes them." If we can get ourselves to the point where we can see past what seems not to be going well in our lives; if we can get ourselves to the point where we absolutely know beyond a shadow of a doubt that the Creative Source always has our best interest at heart, there will be no circumstance for which we will not be grateful.

One of the greatest causes of ingratitude is a fixed mindset. When we have a certain mindset of how things should turn out and they don't turn out that way, it is very easy to become ungrateful. Many times, this occurs as a result of something that is beyond our capacity to change which we refuse to accept or acquiesce to.

The creative channel is a flexible channel. When you are open, it will lead you freely and effortlessly. It is more in a spontaneous state than ever could be in a mechanical state, that we exhibit the God-given power within us. When we let things flow naturally, without forcing our plans on life, we not only create for ourselves peace of mind, we also create for ourselves an opening through which the light of the Divine presence can shine through. And any action performed in this state cannot be mistaken for anything less than the

Creative Source working through us.

Our best bet is to change what we can and accept what we can't, by being grateful for it and not being opposed to it, always bearing in mind that God never lets us pass through any experience that is of no benefit to us. When we channel our lives in this way, we emit gratitude spontaneously in each moment – both for the things we can change and for the things we must surrender to.

Celia Thaxter rightly said, "There is always an eternal summer in the grateful heart."

Gratitude invigorates our bodies. It is a statement of our personality that shows, in a powerful way, our appreciation to God. We were nothing before the Creative Being formed us. Our life is a gift and it is fitting for us, in the least, to offer gratitude for it.

Not only is it important to be grateful for the things already present in your life, you can also be grateful for the things you want to accomplish or attract to your life. As you dream and visualize and work towards achieving your goal, do it in a state of gratitude. Gratitude is the oil that greases the effort we put in to accomplish our dreams and desires. To be grateful is to be graceful.

TYPES OF GRATITUDE

There are many kinds of gratitude and many ways in which we can be genuinely appreciative. They include the following:

1) **GRATITUDE FOR LIFE:** This is the type of gratitude that arises as a result of the things we have already been given directly or

indirectly by the Creative Source. It is gratitude for those things already present in our lives. This type of gratitude is the easiest form of gratitude because it requires no form of work or effort on our part. What we are grateful for already exists in the physical plane.

2) **GRATITUDE FOR GOD MAKING US:** This is the type of gratitude that arises from simply being alive. It is gratitude for who we are. King Solomon once said, "A living dog is better than a dead lion." That's a good summary of this kind of gratitude. This type of gratitude includes, but is not limited to, gratitude for breathing, gratitude for the spontaneous beating of our hearts and gratitude for life in general, in this moment.

3) **GRATITUDE IN SPITE OF CIRCUMSTANCES:** This is the type of gratitude that arises in spite of seemingly negative circumstances that occur in our lives. The awareness that God gives us only what we are capable of handling and that all things work ultimately for our good, makes us understand this kind of gratitude better. This type of gratitude is the hardest form of gratitude, not just because it requires some form of effort or belief on our part, but also because at these times, we literally cannot see anything to be grateful for except through the eyes of faith. It is a type of faith. It is gratitude knowing deep within that all is well even though all doesn't appear to be well.

Indeed challenges can be overwhelming and sometimes very difficult to deal with, yet they ultimately bring out the best in us. It is in the furnace of affliction that diamonds are forged. Every challenge that comes to you is also accompanied by something of great value. And when you are open, by being grateful, you will be able to see past the challenge into the opportunity that is always present. The nature of many challenges tends to disguise the silver lining, yet the silver lining always exists. There is always something of value contained within every challenge. So when life throws a challenge at you, choose to notice the silver lining. Choose to respond rather than react. Choose to see past the challenge into what you can magnificently create. Choose to be grateful in it all.

It is a good idea everyday, to infuse our lives with intermittent injections of gratitude. Gratitude is the oil that greases the wheels of life and makes it run smoother. Gratitude becomes a habit when we consciously choose to make it a part of our daily lives. After a while, it becomes a subconscious habit and we begin to be grateful in all that occurs in our lives without much thought – even for those things that have the face of nothing to be grateful for.

There is so much love and beauty that surrounds you this instant; take a moment to notice it. There is so much colour that is added to your life this day by those people who cherish you and care about you; take a moment to appreciate them. Your life becomes so much deeper and richer when you take time to notice all that is beautiful, delightful and true. Let yourself focus on the beauty that envelopes your world in this moment. Let yourself appreciate all the goodness and loveliness that life has abundantly blessed you with. Let yourself live from a grateful place every moment of every day.

GRATITUDE, THE BEST ANTIDOTE

Gratitude by itself, is an antidote to many evils. Some of these are listed below:

1) **GRATITUDE: THE ANTIDOTE TO DISCONTENT** - If you want to be happy, it is important for you to learn how to be content. If you want to enjoy the gifts and bounties of this life, it is important to be satisfied and appreciative of what you already have.

To be content doesn't mean you make no effort to improve the conditions of your life. To be content means you don't get attached to what you make an effort to improve. It is not your possessions that make you rich; it is who you are. A continual insatiable desire for more is an unhealthy desire. And this has no doubt been the cause of many of the world's current problems. There is no end to craving. If you are always trying to grasp, you lose the natural flow of your life.

Only in a contented and grateful state can you live a life that is filled with grace, beauty and magnificence. Unhealthy desires for things diminish as sincere gratitude for what already exists increases. Life is abundant and is ever ready to share its abundance with and through you.

2) **GRATITUDE: THE ANTIDOTE TO FEAR** – What you fear can rob you of your happiness, erode your joy and keep you from

being the best person you can be. One of the greatest discoveries you can make is to find that your fear is not as overwhelming as it seems to be. One of the greatest discoveries you can make is to become aware of the power you possess to overcome every one of your fears. One obvious way to do this is by thinking about what you are already grateful for.

The longer you think about what you are afraid of, the more it grows. The longer you hide your fear, the stronger it becomes. So instead of cowering in fear, choose to overcome your fear by taking action immediately and you can start to take action immediately by being appreciative of your opportunity for growth. It is by facing your fears that you conquer them, not by evading them. Accept no excuses of yourself. Instead choose to bravely confront your fears with the divine power within you. You gain the strength of every fear you conquer, so keep facing your fears and keep growing stronger.

Just as fears grow stronger by thinking about them, fears diminish by thinking about what you are grateful for. The more appreciative you are, the less fear you will feel. The more appreciative you are, the more able you will be to conquer your fear.

You've been given this amazing tool – gratitude, for you to use anytime, anywhere to combat any kind of fear. Don't hesitate to use it. The more grateful you are, the more fear dissipates. In your thankful state, you can accomplish much more than you ever can in a state of fear.

3) GRATITUDE: THE ANTIDOTE TO IMPRUDENCE – If you are not grateful for what you already have, it is not likely you will be prudent with it. No matter how much you've amassed, it is still good sense to be prudent. No matter how wealthy you've become, it is still good sense not to waste resources. Keep in mind that there are many out there with less who can always benefit from your excess.

Enjoy what you have with the awareness that everything you own is a gift from the Providential Source. Show your appreciation for life by being prudent with it all. You never know if what you waste today will be of immeasurable value to you tomorrow, so learn to be accountable for it all. Have good sense by being prudent. Show good sense by being appreciative. Imprudence results from not taking stock of what already exists in your life. The more you practice gratitude, the less imprudent you will be.

4) GRATITUDE: THE ANTIDOTE TO GREED – Greed is like a wild fire that has gone out of control. It consumes everything in its path and yet is never satisfied. People become greedy when their desire for things gets greater than their need for it. Greed has nothing to do with how financially buoyant you are. It is the spirit behind what you do. Poor people can be greedy too.

It is not in your best interest to desire an improved financial state only for the financial gain or so you can be seen as better than others. Instead, let your aim be for the positive value it can bring to you and to all those who come within your sphere of influence. Gratitude is the sure antidote to greed because it puts a rein on unhealthy appetites.

Bear in mind that no material substance can satisfy the deepest longing of your soul because no material substance was made to do so. Guard yourself from greed by looking around today for things you have you don't really need. Give them away to guard yourself from greed.

GRATITUDE BEYOND FINANCIAL RESOURCES

Many people don't know that there is so much they can be grateful for even without a dime. There is so much money cannot buy that constitutes wealth. Even without millions in your bank account, you can keep the awareness of how rich you really are. Let's explore these together:

1) **YOUR HEALTH:** If you are in good health, you are already abundantly wealthy. Without good health, all the money in the world wouldn't have any meaning. Without good health, you can't really enjoy life. It takes good health to enjoy good (financial) wealth.

2) **YOUR FRIENDS:** True friends are invaluable assets. You cannot buy true friends with money. True friends are those people who stick with you in times of joy and times of sorrow; times of fortune and times of misfortune; times of happiness and times of sadness. Nothing changes their love for you. They are as constant as the sun. Their value is truly immeasurable.

3) **IDEAS/INFORMATION:** Can you place a price tag on information that keeps you from having a heart attack? Or an idea that improves the quality of your life and your relationships? Or an idea that turns you into a multimillionaire? Many of these ideas/information come to you for little or no financial cost, yet their value cannot be underestimated.

4) **TRUE SUCCESS:** As long as you are honoring life in this moment, you are already a successful person. And if you are already successful, you are already wealthy. Don't let a sick world cajole you into believing that success is measured by your accomplishment. It is not end results like reaching a higher position in your company, or earning a certain amount of money or attaining a particular goal that constitutes true success. It is who you are in this moment that makes you successful, not what you have or what you do. The kind of energy you radiate when you work towards these aspirations is what really counts. What you become on the road to your goal is what really matters. That is what cannot be taken away from you.

5) **LIFE:** Without breath, where would be your need for money? Without blood flowing through your veins, what would be the significance of a fat bank account? Life indeed is the greatest wealth. And if you have life, you have hope. With hope, anything is possible.

So in assessing how wealthy you are, remember that wealth encompasses much more than money. Health is wealth. True friends are wealth. Ideas are wealth. True success is wealth and life is the greatest wealth of all. Remember this and be grateful for it all. You cannot be grateful beyond reason because every moment you live is a reason to be grateful.

Sometimes life will box you into a corner leaving you with very limited options. To get out of that corner, begin by being grateful. So much more will come to you in a thankful state than in one of self-pity. There is always something to be thankful for no matter your present predicament. You are living in a rented apartment and your rent is due – someone has been sleeping on the pavement all month. You dislike your job and are advocating for a higher paying one – someone is only wishing they had one. You couldn't buy those new shoes for that remarkable occasion – someone was born without legs.

The best way to live is to be thankful for what you have while you aim for the things you hope for. When you notice the already blooming flowers at your feet, you reach your goals easier and quicker.

The thing about gratitude is that it always opens up more doors for more things to come your way. Gratitude refreshes and invigorates your soul. When things don't seem to be going your way, and you choose to be genuinely grateful, your sincere act is registered and things immediately begin to work in your favour. You are never short of things to be grateful for if you take the time to look for them. Let your mind focus on these and keep yourself in a constant state of gratitude.

WAYS OF SHOWING GRATITUDE TO OTHERS

1) **ATTENTION:** Give whoever you are with, the gift of your full attention. When you are attentive to others, you bring rich value to them and great value to life. Your attention shows that you genuinely appreciate them. In giving your full attention to them, you participate with them in a total, undivided and whole way. You let them know how important, special and loved they are by the gift of your attention.

Not only is this kind of full undivided attention important to give to others, it is also important to give to yourself. Give your full attention to everything you do and you will notice how much better you do them. When you give your full attention to the details of your daily life, even to the most trivial things, you are in that moment honoring life and when you honor life, you will be rewarded. God always appreciates those who remember to show appreciation for life.

2) **GENUINE APPRECIATION:** When someone does something for you, show your appreciation. Even if they didn't do it exactly as you would have liked them to, appreciate their effort. Appreciation is the grease that oils the wheels of relationships. When you appreciate people, you make them feel better about themselves and in turn also make yourself feel better.

Ralph Waldo Emerson once said, "It is one of the most beautiful compensations of this life that no man can sincerely try to help another without helping himself." And Zig Ziglar quipped, "You can get all you want in life, if you help enough other people get what they want."

People can tell when what you say is really true or if you have an ulterior motive so don't bother flattering anyone. Flattery pushes people away. Appreciation draws them close. People love appreciation that is sincere, direct and heart-felt. The more you appreciate people, the more you make them want to do things which will make you appreciate them more.

3) **ACTS OF KINDNESS:** Anytime you perform any act of kindness, no matter how small, you set in motion a Law that causes you to be the recipient of the very thing you offer. Anytime you give from your heart in tangible and intangible ways, you truly enrich others and at the same time, enrich yourself. Your giving opens your heart and makes you receptive to the graces contained within your divine spirit.

Your gift directly affects your heart. And as you keep being a channel of blessing to others, God will open up channels that will cause others to be a blessing to you. The nature of the world is such that you are always at an advantage to someone in some way, so utilize this opportunity, not as an opening for arrogance but as an opening to be of service to others.

Circumstances will never be perfect but you can perfect each moment by showing your appreciation for it. Everything you aspire to become is directly affected by everything you are now. If you want a beautiful tomorrow, then make a genuine effort to create a beautiful today. You can begin to create that by being grateful for your current circumstances.

BENEFITS OF GRATITUDE

Just as a plant or flower starts to wither and die when it stops growing, people begin to depreciate when they stop appreciating. Gratitude is an essential part of living. When you are grateful, you not just become better, you also become happier.

Gratitude causes expansion, not contraction; growth not stagnation; progression, not regression. Your life can be so much better if you incorporate gratitude into everything you do.

Here are a few things being grateful does:

1) **IMPROVES CREATIVITY:** Gratitude improves creativity because it opens up the channel that connects you with the Divine. When you are grateful for what you create, you send a clear signal for more avenues to be created for you to utilize your God-given talents. Those who make gratitude a constant part of their lives find that they are able to create better and become so much more efficient. We are made in the image of God and so we have creative potential within us. This potential can be activated by being grateful for the gifts, talents and capacities God has endowed us with. Gratitude truly awakens you to inner creativity.

2) **HELPS YOU COPE BETTER WITH CHALLENGES:** People who incorporate gratitude in their daily lives find that they are

better able to cope with the inevitable delays and challenges that come with normal living. Life does not always go the way you like. It is gratitude that has the power to turn days that are disappointing into a delightful experience. People who are grateful are able to see roses in thorns, rainbows in storms and bright sunrays through darkened cloud forms. Gratitude illuminates your path so you don't stumble in the dark when you pass through it.

When going through a challenge, people who are without gratitude are less likely to be positively minded and persistent and this adversely affects the outcome of their experience. Those who are grateful are able to do so knowing that what they are going through won't last forever. They know that the tunnel does not remain dark endlessly and that there is always light at the end of it.

If there were no challenges, there would be no growth. Challenges cause some people to become bitter while causing others to become better. Those who see challenges in the right light are those who become better. Those who see nothing in them to be grateful for are those who become bitter.

3) **DEEPENS YOUR CONNECTION WITH GOD:** There is nothing that you have which you have not been graciously given by the Source of all things. There is nothing that exists in your world which has not been graciously made available to you by the Supreme Being. If you take an honest look at the conditions and place of your birth, your kind of parents, your genetic make-up, your experiences and opportunities, you will see that so much good has come to you

that is way beyond your ordinary capacity. Grateful people are constantly aware of this and this draws them closer to God. Gratitude incites humility in us and pushes pride far away. What would you be able to claim as your own if all that lies beyond your control were taken away from you?

There is more to every single activity carried out than is visible. There is so much behind the scenes that you are absolutely unaware of. If you are really honest with yourself, you would see that many of the things that had to go right for your plans to be established were way beyond your control. By being grateful to God, you cause yourself to be the recipient of many more things to be grateful for.

4) **MAKES YOU MORE LOVING:** Earlier in this chapter, I already talked about gratitude being the best antidote. Gratitude makes you a happier person and so much more loving. Gratitude keeps you from being discontented by letting you take stock of how much you already have. Gratitude conquers fear because when you are grateful, you become more loving and love casts out fear.

Fear is a type of suffering which seldom comes to those who are grateful. And when it does come to them, they are easily able to tackle it by flooding their awareness with things to be grateful for. Gratitude makes you prudent and makes you a master of your resources. These preserved resources can then be used for the benefit of many others who will be very appreciative of the love you've shown to them. Gratitude makes you see the material world for what it really is. It helps you realize that resources are simply tools for self-improvement and for the betterment of mankind.

5) **IMPROVES YOUR IMMUNE SYSTEM:** The kinds of thoughts you think directly affect your physical body. Thoughts of sickness and disease can make your body sick and diseased. On the other hand, thoughts of wholeness and vitality make your body healthy and vibrant. Thoughts of gratitude are always healthy and positive thoughts which inspire good feelings which in turn affect how your body responds. Always think grateful thoughts and expect more things to be grateful for.

Take a scenario of two people who develop a common cold. One person thinks of all the symptoms and signs of the disease, looks at all the adverse effects of the drugs being used and is afraid of their effects. The other person is aware of the symptoms and the signs of the disease, but does not dwell on them. This person is grateful that the condition is not worse than it already is and lives fully believing that 'this too shall pass.' Which of these two people do you think is going to make a quicker recovery? The answer is obvious, isn't it?

6) **IMPROVES SLEEP:** People who are grateful naturally get better sleep because they infuse gratitude into their daily schedules. Those who just before going to bed, think of or write down things that occurred during their day for which they are grateful are far more likely to have a more enjoyable sleep. People who are grateful are less likely to worry because they have already replaced their worrisome thoughts with thoughts of gratitude. Those who ceaselessly worry

about how to pay the bills or their children's school fees or how to meet the needs of their spouses are less likely to feel grateful for what they already have and are less likely to sleep soundly.

When your connection to the Divine Source is strengthened through gratitude, you begin to trust completely, eliminating worry as you function at your peak. People who effectively utilize their day tend to sleep better at night. The gratitude pill does more for you than any sleeping pill could ever do. The more gratitude pills you take, the less sleeping pills you'll require.

7) **DEEPENS YOUR RELATIONSHIPS:** Gratitude improves your relationships and makes them more enjoyable. It is very easy to become too familiar with a mate, friend, or companion or anyone who forms a significant part of your life. It is very easy to let things slip and become complacent. Gratitude guards against this. It helps you step back from yourself and from your routine way of seeing things so that you can see with a renewed insight. Familiarity makes people take many things for granted. They let the habitual pattern of daily living prevent them from seeing the true beauty of their relationships.

A good way to prevent this is to periodically make a list of things you love about the people in your life and are grateful for. Remember all the unique and amazing qualities they possess that bring rich value to you. Remember how much more brightly your world shines because they are a part of it.

8) **INCREASES PRODUCTIVITY:** Gratitude makes you more productive and also encourages productivity in others. Those who are grateful for the goals they have already achieved are more likely to achieve more goals. Gratitude boosts your energy and enhances your courage to attempt and accomplish greater things.

Charles Schwab said, "I have yet to find the man, however exalted his station, who did not do better work and put forth greater effort under a spirit of approval than under a spirit of criticism." When you approve of people by letting them know how grateful you are for their contribution, you make them want to contribute even more. The more admirable qualities you recognize in them, the more admirable qualities they will want to exhibit. Sometimes, however, criticism is not only advisable but necessary. This, nevertheless, should be done in a healthy way. It should be done in a spirit of love with the intention to build up, not to tear down.

9) **MAKES YOU MORE ATTRACTIVE:** The more appreciative you are, the nicer and more attractive you become. The more appreciative you are, the more people will want to trust you. When you appreciate your spouse, she'll want to do even more things you can appreciate her for. When you appreciate your children, they'll break their limits just so you can appreciate them again.

Gratitude builds bridges between people and knits them closely together. You are more likely to come across unexpected, amazing opportunities when you are constantly in a state of gratitude because you not only become more attractive to others, you also develop a more attractive personality. People who are constantly in a state of gratitude are more likely to have quality friends and an enhanced social life. This in turn leads to more openings which further reinforces their sense of gratitude.

Gratitude makes you more gracious and polite. People who are grateful are less likely to be nasty or have an unpleasant attitude towards others.

10) **ENHANCES YOUR SELF-ESTEEM:** Another significant benefit of gratitude is that it enhances your self esteem while also improving your character. People who regularly practise gratitude are less likely to be material-minded because their focus is on those things they already can be grateful for. Gratitude makes you more jovial, uplifts your spirit and makes you feel worthy.

Low self-esteem comes from not being able to appreciate yourself and the unique qualities and abilities you possess. It comes from focusing on the negatives. Gratitude directly combats this because it makes you more appreciative of those things that make you different and unique. Gratitude helps you keep stock of where you are relative to where you have been. It helps you keep track of your previous accomplishments, thereby boosting your self-confidence and increasing your self-esteem.

If you take time to reflect, you will notice that so much is different for you now than it was last week or last month or last year. Gratitude helps you value yourself and value others too. When you are aware of the positive value you bring to others and to life in general, your self-esteem soars. Gratitude is the perfect antidote for times when you are feeling down or disillusioned. When you place your attention back on what you are grateful for, you are then able to see that life is not as bad as it seems and then you are able to bounce back much quicker.

A PERSONAL EXPERIENCE

A few years ago, I was in a place I like to call "redundant". This happened because life was not what I was used to anymore. Ingratitude tried to creep into my heart and poison me with its fangs.

So I began a "Journal of Thanks" on the 27th day of June, 2007 which I kept up for many months. I found something everyday for which I was grateful and wrote it down. To this day, that simple act has totally transformed my life because it made me look at familiar things in a new light, made me feel better about myself and others and caused more blessings to pour into my life for which I am very grateful.

I began the Journal with the following words: "I begin this 'Journal of Thanks' today because I believe it is so easy to forget the numerous blessings You bestowed and still bestow on me while concentrating on problems that exist presently or potential problems which will not be made any easier by fretting."

I now have the memory of this experience and often refer back to it. And when I experience any degree of redundancy, I know immediately I have been concentrating too much on problems and it is time to switch my mind over to a state of gratitude.

Those who make gratitude a fundamental part of their existence find that they have the courage to jump over the hurdles of life by propelling themselves forward with joy and grace. Those who practice gratitude become what they practice, they become grateful people and this completely changes their perspective and attitude towards life.

9

NON-JUDGMENT: THE ROUTE TO CREATIVITY

"Judge not and you will not be judged. For with the judgment you use, you will be judged. And with the measure you use, you will be measured." ~ Matt 7:1-2

Aside from the ego which is a huge inhibitor of inborn creativity, judging others also hinders the force of the Divine from flowing freely through you. The Creator works through you when you are open. Judgment barricades this link and diminishes or completely impedes the Divine Presence from flowing freely through you. The more layers of judgment you have, the less creative you'll be.

The world functions on the premise of giving and receiving, so what you put out is what eventually comes back to you, whether you are conscious of it or not. Jesus said in the gospel of Matthew that those who judge will be judged and the way you judge others is the way you will be judged.

By this, He did not mean to approve the old way of judging, which is "an eye for an eye", but intended to demonstrate to us a higher way. He showed that it is only in a state of living without judgment that we are free from being judged.

When you live in a non-judgmental way, you not only love others better, you also love yourself better and become a prime example of forgiveness.

Many diseases that develop are caused by an inability to truly love and not primarily by external factors. People who constantly judge others are more susceptible to diseases and illnesses of various kinds.

It is important to learn to see yourself as God sees you, not as people see you. Remember that people are entitled to their own opinions and just because a person thinks "a" or says "b" about you doesn't mean it has to affect or characterize you. Let yourself embark on the journey beginning today that leads to the place where people's thoughts about you do not define or control you.

Instead of judging yourself, choose to appreciate your unique and amazing qualities. Choose to see yourself in your true light; not less than or greater than who you are. Do not stop shining your brightest simply because someone else is unhappy about it. Don't let other people's perception of your light frighten you. Don't allow the light of others to frighten you either.

In our true essence, we are all one. I am my brother and my brother is me. The less we judge ourselves and others, the more love we can manifest in the world and the better we can show that God's power resides within us.

SCALES OF JUDGMENT

Judging takes place based on various scales. The three main scales are described below:

1) **PRIVATE JUDGMENT:** Judgment can occur when individuals decide to privately enact judgment on their own. When this happens, they block true creativity from freely expressing itself through them. Mahatma Gandhi once said, "An eye for an eye leaves the whole world blind." If every individual were to enact private judgment for every perceived or real wrong, then we would be left in a dark world where the cycle of revenge keeps spiraling.

2) **INSTITUTIONAL JUDGMENT:** The most recognized way of enacting judgment in the world is through institutions. Here, judges are assigned to pass judgment on the cases they preside on. Although these judges are just like you and I, they are given the prerogative by virtue of their profession to judge. These judges help to maintain stability in the world.

Various courts are set up to listen and ultimately pass judgment on people who have committed a crime (real or perceived). But due to the fallible nature of humans, judges are not always perfect in enacting judgment. Even their most honest efforts may be clouded by emotions and a subconscious predisposition of one party over another. In the Law Court, what is reckoned as true is not necessarily what is true but what can be proven to be true.

3) **DIVINE JUDGMENT:** The most universal, though least acknowledged way judgment takes place is through the Divine means. The Creative Source has a stamp on everything. A clay pot is made by a potter, a brick house is made by a bricklayer and a painting is made by an artist. Regardless of what the items are used for, they each bear the stamp of their maker. Similarly, The Creator stamps a unique quality on everything that is made regardless of what it is used for.

The reason why God is a better judge than man is that God has all the details, knows all the history and is the silent unbiased witness to all conversations including those that reside in heart. God is not swayed by personal opinion and does not give preference to any single individual but judges everyone on the same scale.

Ralph Waldo Emerson once wrote, "I cannot see what you see, because I am caught up by a strong wind, and blown so far in one direction that I am out of the hoop of your horizon." Not only does judgment impede the creative spark in each of us, it also obstructs our true vision. Judgment makes us see people not as they are but as we perceive them to be. So much untold assistance gets diverted off our path when we choose to see through the lens of judgment.

TYPES OF JUDGING

1) **PHYSICAL JUDGMENT:** This type of judgment results in an outward expression of retaliation for a perceived wrong done by

another person. Sometimes this judgment may be warranted but we are never in a position to pass judgment on another individual. By passing judgment on another, we are in effect saying we can do it all by ourselves, and so do not desire God's backing. This is the most common type of judgment. It is shown by an outward expression of the inner dissatisfaction we feel for another person. When we try to push others down the hill of judgment, our hands are glued to our sides and we tumble down the same hill ourselves.

2) **MENTAL JUDGMENT:** In this type of judgment, we label people in our heads. This does not always translate to physical judgment but is always where physical judgment begins from. Here a person thinks in the head about things done or perceived to be done by another individual. These thoughts become commentaries in the head that can last for hours, days, months and sometimes even years. Mentally judging causes all sorts of negative emotions to build up that impedes the natural creative process.

This kind of judgment causes harm to us in more ways than we realize because in the end, we are the ones who end up being judged and are not able to see the ones we judge clearly for who they really are. This results in a dense vibration that limits our ability to fully express our inborn creativity.

It was Mark Twain who said, "Anger is an acid that can do more harm to the vessel in which it is stored than to anything on which it is poured." And Bob Marley adds, "Emancipate yourself from mental slavery. None but ourselves can free our minds."

When we pass judgment on another, we imprison ourselves by ourselves. The chains that we use to bind the hands and feet of others also bind our own hand and feet too. You will be measured on the same scale you use to measure others. You will be judged by in the same way you judge others.

3) **UNCONSCIOUS JUDGMENT:** This is a type of judgment that occurs on a subliminal level. It is unconscious because we are not mentally aware of making the judgment. It is different from the other types of judgment because here, we unconsciously label another individual. We become aware of this type of judgment when we reflect on our outward, overt actions.

How we act towards other people gives us feedback on whether we have judged them internally or not. An unconscious judgment is not only one that sees another human being as less important but also one that looks at a human being as more important. Certainly, this does not mean that respect should not be given to whom respect is due, but that we should realize that our own essence is the same as the essence of any other person.

The irony of this type of judgment is that even in an unconscious state, you will still suffer the consequences of your unconscious acts. The world is built on the Law of cause and effect and you being unaware of your judgment does not, in any way, minimize its consequences. Emerson rightly said, "Life is a series of lessons that has to be lived to be understood."

LISTENING WITHOUT JUDGING

Most people listen with the intent of saying something back in return. Few people truly listen without this intention. Even fewer listen with complete awareness, devoid of any preceding judgment on the thing being said. When you live on a non-judmental plane, even your mere listening can be healing to the one you converse with, because there is a lightness that is easily felt and absorbed by the people you converse with. Your mind is free from judgment and is open. When your mind is open, your heart will be open. The key to a compassionate heart is a mind that is completely free of judgment.

Edward Chapin said, "Do not judge men by appearances; for the light laughter that bubbles on the lip often mantles over depths of sadness and the serious look may be the sober veil that covers a divine peace and joy." Our basic and natural instinct is to make a quick judgment on the people we meet but many times, this judgment is flawed because of an incomplete knowledge or erroneous perception.

Many people form opinions of other people at face value based on first impression but both face value and first impression can be very misleading. We lose so much when we do not take time to reflect on the true essence of another human being. We lose so much when we do not take time to understand people.

Jesus said in the book of Matthew, "For to the one who has, more will be given, and he will have an abundance, but from the one who has not, even what he has will be taken away from him". This statement also applies to judging.

The one who keeps on judging others becomes more paranoid. Everyone they meet begin to look suspicious. After living in this way for a while, they create a prison for themselves and build up tough defenses for themselves where no real danger exists.

If you make even the tiniest effort to refrain from judging others, more grace will be given to you to judge less and more space will be created for you to shine in your true essence. Anything that causes the density of your mind to lessen or diminishes your ego or enables you to truly listen to another human being without judging, causes your creativity to grow and glow, lighting up your entire world in the process.

We always see more clearly from a non-judgmental point of view. Not only do we see more clearly, the clarity with which we see is also seen by others.

The type of creativity that comes through you when you are open and free of thoughts of judgment is one that originates from a higher plane than the physical. There is a place in each person's soul that yearns for authenticity; a place that yearns for the authenticity in me to be noticed by the authenticity in you and where this link is made, there is a magnificent connection of one soul to another.

As you practice non-judgment everyday, you gradually begin to awaken to your inborn creativity. As your creativity flourishes, your soul gets refreshed. You become a vessel, a harbinger, a channel for true divinity in the world.

NON-JUDGEMENT AND FORGIVENESS

Jesus' words on the cross, "Father, forgive them for they know not what they do" are a prime example of what it means to live without judgment. To forgive means to 'look through' or to 'overlook'. Jesus knew that the people who committed such heinous crimes against him were unconscious. He knew that if they truly knew who they were and who he was, they would not have done what they did.

He saw them for who they really were and not just what they seemed to be. He chose to look through all the layers of density that made them unconscious. He saw their true essence.

Non-judgment is a type of forgiveness because anytime you choose to look through or overlook someone else's actions, you are choosing to live in love. However, as I said before, looking through or overlooking people's actions doesn't mean people become unaccountable for their actions because of ignorance. They are still responsible and will still face the consequences of their actions despite their lack of awareness.

Note also that to forgive doesn't mean you become a doormat for someone else to trample upon. To forgive doesn't mean you have to keep an offender in your life either. Forgiveness is necessary, but association is by choice.

Remember, you alone are responsible for healing your life. You alone are responsible for the quality of life you live so free yourself of the burden that unforgiveness brings and allow yourself to live a powerful and complete life.

WHO IS NON-JUDGMENT FOR?

1) **FOR YOURSELF:** There are many things you have done in the past that you would not have done if only you knew better then. It's okay to regret past actions as long as you can learn from them. The problem arises when you begin to hold on to your past regrets to the extent that the heaviness of it clouds the aliveness of your present moment.

With your present level of awareness, you should be able to look through your past. Forgive yourself because you didn't know what you were doing then. People who say, "Because of what I did, I will never forgive myself" do not know the true meaning of living without judgment. Not until they release themselves from all forms of self-judgment can they become truly free. When you do not judge yourself, you open up your creative channels.

Forgiveness is not complete until you are able to see yourself without judgment. You are who you are, not who you were. Yes, who you were contributed to making you the person you are today, but if you continually keep looking at who you were, you imprison yourself to do only things you've done in the past and impede your chances of living a truly creative and successful life in this moment.

2) **FOR OTHERS:** Different people are at different levels of consciousness and it is from their level of consciousness that they act. If someone truly believes in his heart that something is right (even if it is clearly wrong), he lives what is true for him until his awareness

grows to where he is able to see beyond his current plane. Though he may have acted in error, to him, in that moment, that error is his truth.

So many people have done things that were unthinkable and unbelievable to other human beings. Many of them were not even aware of the gravity of their actions when they did them, but became conscious later on as their awareness grew.

The beginning of sanity in the world is not just in taking active steps to make the outside world a better place, but also in taking active steps to make your inner world better.

If everyone concentrated on raising their awareness, half of the world's problems would be solved. The world begins to correct itself when you begin to correct yourself. The influence you can exert on the world is limited, but the influence you can exert on yourself has no limits. As you free yourself from blame and judgment and release others through forgiveness, the world gets freed as well.

3) **FOR HUMANITY:** Next, non-judgment is for humanity as a whole. When you look at history, it is not difficult to see the madness that has ravaged the world. So many examples abound of the deep madness that envelops the world. From the world wars to the present day senseless killings that take place sporadically everyday; from Hitler of Germany to Bashar al-Assad of Syria; from the thousands dying of starvation in Somalia to the corrupt and despicable practices that exist in many parts of sub-Saharan Africa. And the list goes on and on.

It is easy to get angry and keep that anger in you in the name of carrying the justice of the world on your shoulders, but think about what this really does to you. What does it do to your state of consciousness? Anger and any other kind of negative emotion kept in your heart doesn't make the world better; it only adds to the madness of it.

Do what you can in your own sphere of influence and the world immediately begins to correct itself. It immediately begins to right itself. Unless you are able to look through the madness and the most heinous atrocities, you will not be able to grow in compassion and say like Jesus did, "Father, forgive them for they know not what they do." Certainly this does not mean that atrocities should go unpunished but that you are able to see through the atrocities that have been committed.

As you improve your world by creatively allowing your light to shine, the world improves as well. As you concentrate your energies on the one person you can control – yourself, you take back your power to change the world. By shifting from a plane of anger and resentment to a plane of love and compassion, the world begins to feel the impact and begins to change itself.

NON-JUDGMENT IN RELATIONSHIPS

Non-judgment is directly applicable to all kinds of relationships. You see, non-judging is not just a type of forgiveness but also a type of love. When you are able to look through your spouse or your parents or your children, what fills your heart is a deep sense of compassion and empathy for them regardless of what they have or haven't done in the physical plane.

Judgment affects our perception of people especially those closest to us. When you look at your spouse through the lenses of judgment, your perception is clouded and your vision is obscured. You cannot see behind whatever misdeed or wrong is perceived to have been done. But when you are able to look through, you create the kind of atmosphere that is characteristic of true love and exhibit a type of grace that is unique and distinct to you.

The arguments and misunderstandings that occur regularly in marriages and close relationships are largely due to an inability to overlook offenses. Ralph Marston Jr. said, "Let go of your attachment to being right, and suddenly your mind is more open. You're able to benefit from the unique view points of others, without being crippled by your own judgment." The mind is open when it is not clouded by judgment. The feeling that your way and your way alone is the right way without bringing the view points of others into consideration is not the best way to live.

There are no perfect humans, only humans striving for perfection. When you realize that you are not perfect yourself and that you have also made mistakes in the past, it opens your heart to be able to be more tolerant and understanding of others.

Love is the truth. Love is the answer. Love is the way. I wish I could say this enough times but I myself am a work in progress and an active student of what is written through me. The Buddha quipped, "As rain falls on the just and the unjust, do not burden your heart with judgments but rain your kindness equally on all." And Mother Teresa said, "When you judge people, you have no time to love them."

Judgment burdens the heart, weighs down the soul and impedes true creativity. If you truly love someone, then there will be no room for judgment. Relationships become heaven on earth when the purity that comes from being like God infuses and invigorates them.

Don't be too quick to judge someone's motives because you never know why or for what purpose they do what they do. Don't stifle the natural flow of your life by clouding it with bias judgments on others. There are many reasons why people do what they do and their reasons may be beyond your immediate ability to comprehend.

There are a myriad of ways in which non-judgment improves and sustains relationships. When you are able to look through your partner or your spouse or your parent, you will easily be able to do all the following which will make your relationship richer:

1) **BE PATIENT WITH THEM:** Through the eyes of non-judgment, a lot of evil, injury and provocation can be appropriately dealt with without feelings of resentment, revenge or indignation. For example, when a partner is not functioning at their best for certain reasons, and you are able to look through that and offer forgiveness, you enhance the quality of your relationship. The sacredness of your relationship gets preserved because you acknowledge that the injuries and misdeeds that sometimes occur in the relationship are not greater than the relationship itself.

2) **AVOID ENVY:** A person who is in a state of non-judgment will easily be able to appreciate the unique qualities of a partner or spouse. They will not discount or feel intimidated by any of the good qualities their partner possesses. A person who lives in a state of non-judgment will see the essence of an individual before the qualifications of the individual. It is this true connection that should be encouraged.

3) **NOT GET EASILY ANGRY WITH THEM:** Anger cannot stay where non-judgment resides. And where anger cannot be avoided, passions are effectively restrained in a person who is free from judgment. Certainly, anger can occur in a person with genuine love, but it does not reside there. It is human and natural to be angry but very few people are angry at the right time and for the right reasons. Very few people know how to control their anger and even fewer, know when they have crossed the danger line.

4) **BELIEVE THE BEST OF THEM:** In a state of non-judgment, you will always be willing to believe the best of your partner or spouse. You will not let your mind be clouded by undue or inappropriate suspicion without definite or substantial proof. You will encourage the good qualities in your partner so that they can grow to fill your home. You will lovingly correct your partner without making an enemy of them or recollecting previous faults on present occasions.

With non-judgment also comes wisdom and this affects the

quality of your relationship. Certainly, believing the best of another person doesn't necessarily mean you become free of all doubts, but that you live in a state where your first thought of them is one of approval and not one of suspicion.

5) **NOT SUPPOSE GOOD ACTIONS COME FROM BAD MOTIVES:** Anything that causes your judgment to become clouded will naturally inhibit the divine creativity that is your birthright. If you think that the good your partner does comes from a bad motive, then you shortchange yourself by constraining the many ways your partner can be truly useful to you. In a state of non-judgment, a good action performed will not be believed to come from a bad motive. When suspicion exists in relationships, it grows to poison the relationship and a relationship that was once blissful and beautiful becomes one that is unbearable and filled with apprehension because a necessary ingredient of the relationship – trust, was lost. There is no relationship that will not function more effectively and efficiently when non-judgment defines it.

JUDGMENT BY APPEARANCES

Gold does not always glitter and what glitters may be hollow and empty inside. People are very often better or worse than their face value. A lot of atrocities are committed when people are taken for what they seem to be and not for who they really are.

David L. Weatherford said, "A flower that is not the prettiest in the garden may yet have the loveliest fragrance." The prettiest face does not always equate with the most beautiful soul. A person can have a wrinkled and deformed body and yet have a heart as beautiful, innocent and pure as that of a child.

Abraham Lincoln once said, "I do not like that man. I must get to know him better." Indeed, this is one American President who didn't judge by appearances because he was determined to see through people to their true essence.

No one should be written off. A physical birth alone is enough proof that God has need for that soul here. Many of those who have been written off as those who had little or nothing to offer, are those who have eventually gone on to become great men and women of society.

Give people time to learn better ways of doing things. We are all different and function best in different ways. Be patient with people. Give them time so they can marvel you with their competence and amazing skills.

Gerald Jampolsky said, 'When I am able to resist the temptation to judge others, I can see them as teachers of forgiveness in my life, reminding me that I can only have peace of mind when I forgive, rather than judge."

HOW TO BREAK FREE OF JUDGMENT

How can you break free from a continual cycle of judgment and live a life of non-judgment so that creativity can flow freely through you?

The first thing to note is that God is always for you and never against you and that everything happens for you, not to you. Again,

Apostle Paul in the book of Romans said "And we know with great confidence that God who is deeply concerned about us causes all things to work together as a plan for good for those who love God, to those who are called according to His plan and purpose."

The following steps can be followed to free yourself of judgment.

1) **OBSERVE:** The first step is to observe. Notice when you make judgments. What you cannot see, you cannot change. If you are always blind to your own judging, you will not see a need to correct yourself. You've got to be able to observe judgment in yourself to be able to transcend it. Without seeing judgment for what it is, you cannot become free of it.

2) **ACKNOWLEDGE:** The next step is to acknowledge. Admit the part of yourself that judges. Acknowledge that whenever you lose your creative connection, you are in that moment not as loving as you should be. Come to terms with it. Be able to see that it is not just a personal problem but a collective problem of humanity that arises from the ego. Acknowledge your desire to be free from judging.

Nancy Lopez said, "Doubt yourself and you doubt everything you see. Judge yourself and you see judges everywhere. But if you listen to the sound of your own voice, you can rise above doubt and judgment. And you can see forever."

3) **RELEASE THOUGHTS OF JUDGMENT:** Forgive yourself.

Forgive others. Forgive the world. Release thoughts of judgment. Forgive by simply deciding to let go. One way you can do that is by being fully present. When you live wholly in the moment, then you are not constrained by the events that occurred in the past or improperly drawn to events that are yet to occur. Your full attention is in the moment and so it becomes easier for you, in that instant, to become free of judgment. The more present you are, the less judgmental you will be.

4) **BRING YOURSELF BACK:** The final step is to bring yourself back to your creative center anytime you catch yourself making a biased or inappropriate judgment on another. Certainly you are a human being and are bound to slip up sometimes. If and when you do, do not beat yourself up over and over again, instead release all thoughts of judgment and bring yourself back to your creative plane. Allow the Spirit of God to illuminate your whole being by asking for forgiveness so that you can be a pure conduit for manifestation of divine creativity.

10

PROTECT YOUR DREAM

"To be nobody but yourself in a world that's doing its best to make you somebody else, is to fight the hardest battle you are ever going to fight and never stop fighting." ~ E.E. Cummings

In our present society, mediocrity is the lowest common denominator. The light of creativity easily gets obscured by other people who will stop at nothing to make you like them. Society is averse to individuality. It is averse to originality. It is those who have forgotten the song that sings in their soul that will do everything humanly possible to make you forget your own song.

The authenticity and originality that is characteristic of true creativity cannot be mistaken or taken for something that it is not. Anytime you live fearlessly from your heart, it is an obvious reminder to others of what they ought to be doing and a cue to how they haven't been true to themselves.

The thing about being like somebody else is that you can never fully really represent that person. It is like leaving your own perfectly sized dress and trying to wear one that is too big or too small for you. People who try to be like other people deny the world of their creative uniqueness and deny themselves of their creative capacity to fully express themselves.

People cannot know for certain who you are because your life is obscured and not yet congruent with who you were created to be.

If you want to live a creative life, it is important to guard your creativity. If you want to fully express yourself, it is important to be mindful and watchful of any weed that tries to crop up in your beautiful garden. These weeds can be thoughts and words from well-meaning people who think they know what is best for you. But who can know the song that sings in your own heart better than the one that owns it and the One that created it?

Ralph Waldo Emerson said, "The power which resides in you is new in nature, and none but you know what it is you can do, nor can you know till you have tried." There are levels of creativity that will remain locked inside you until you courageously choose to open your creative doors, regardless of how frightened you are. As you live from your creative center everyday, you open up more doors that lead to many more creative places.

It is by being yourself that you discover who you really are. The more you try to imitate another person, the farther away from your creative center you drift. What will give you true peace and fulfillment is choosing to live from your authentic space. How will you know this? You will know. Your heart will tell you. You will be joyously and creatively alive and be validated when you are living from your creative center.

A lot of people try to drown the dream of their heart by becoming addicted to drinks, drugs and sex. Some others try to drown theirs by performing various selfless services to humanity but not until you are living wholly from your creative place can you truly know peace.

Nothing else will do. You were cut from a particular cloth and no one else can do what you are made to do. No one else can successfully serve your purpose. It is for you and you alone.

Alan Ashley-Pitt said, "The man who follows the crowd will usually get no further than the crowd. The man who walks alone is likely to find himself in places no one has ever been before." Certainly, no man is an island. No one succeeds alone. We all need people. However Ashley-Pitt makes a vital point when seen from a creative perspective. You cannot find out who you truly are if you keep following the crowd. Only as you bravely take what rightly belongs to you can you truly achieve the real progress that your heart desires. By maintaining your distinctiveness, you create the opening for you to become all that you are meant to be.

Living a creative life is not a walk in the park. Living creatively is choosing to swim with the undertow instead of the current of the crowd. The challenges you will face are real and many but the journey is always worth the challenge.

GUARD YOUR HEART

To protect your dream, it is important that you are mindful of the influences that come into your life. To protect your dream, it is important to guard your heart. The opinions of other people about you are as fickle as the blowing of the wind or the caption of a daily newspaper. They can change at any moment. If you let other people's thoughts about you be the guiding factor in your life, you will be left to their whims and moods. You will have no control over your life and you will be like a ship tossed to and fro in the deep blue sea with no pilot to set the sails. It is far worse to lose the validation of your heart than it is to lose the validation of others.

The apostle Paul in the book Romans says, "If possible, as far as it depends on you, live at peace with everyone.". Take advice but don't let anyone order you around. If what they advice goes contrary to the song in your heart. Break yourself free. You will only find true happiness when you swim with the tide of your own heart.

Your goal should be to reach the point where neither praise nor criticism can change you. Your goal should be to reach the point where you are unfazed by both noble and negative reports about you. You goal should be to reach the place where you keep on being true to yourself no matter what anyone else thinks or says. It is not your business to concern yourself with the thoughts of others. Your business is to guard your heart. The quality of your thoughts determines the quality of your life so don't let anyone "walk through your mind with their dirty feet," as Mahatma Ghandi rightly quipped.

YOUR AUTHENTIC SELF

You are a unique and magnificent being. You were born original and authentic, so choose to remain so. Your originality is where your gifting lies so choose to use it to make the best of your life and the lives of those around you. You can only be yourself fully, so don't bother trying to be anyone else. As long as you have a sincere desire and are making an honest effort to know yourself, you will be assisted by life at every turn. By choosing to be somebody else, you misrepresent yourself.

There is so much creative richness inside you so use it to the best of your ability. It is your fail-proof arsenal. Allow the beam that shines from the Divine to flow freely through you and let everything you say and do resound with the original you.

As you keep being your authentic self, your authenticity flows into every smile, every gesture and every word. It flows into everything you do. People who observe you will notice the grace and beauty which your life exudes because you choose to be true to yourself. The only way you can truly bloom is to truly be yourself.

ASSOCIATIONS DETERMINE ALTITUDE

Your associations matter. Your associations determine your altitude. Without the right kind of people surrounding you, you will not be able to live the dream of your heart. Without the right kind of advice, you will be cajoled into thinking that what everyone else is doing is what you should be doing.

When a dream is born within you, the potential for its realization is also born. The persons you associate with will determine how fast your dream will take flight. Because we are human beings, we are all susceptible to the influences of those we surround ourselves with. You cannot be with another person for a prolonged period of time and not be affected by them. You become like those you associate with whether you like it or not.

There will always be those who do not live true to themselves but then there are also those who live true to themselves and others. By associating with the right group of people, you reinforce and strengthen the dream of your heart. By associating with the right group of people, you support, nurture and care for yourself.

Certainly, there will always be those who will laugh at your dream, ridicule it or deride it. There will be those who will try to crush it. Yet if this dream is truly yours, if it comes from the place in your heart that cannot be touched by the world, hold on to it. Do not let the firmly planted but tender roots of your dream be uprooted by winds of disapproval or disdain. Don't let anyone steal your dream because if you do, from that moment, you stop being true to yourself and begin to misrepresent your soul.

So let the vision of your dream coming true spur you onwards and forwards to a delightful and beautiful achievement. Let the fulfillment that comes with purposeful accomplishment drive you on.

Be careful about those you share your dream with, especially in its early stages. Choose to associate with high-minded individuals who listen to the call of their creative spirit. You do yourself a favour anytime you engage in any activity that helps you become more genuine. It is only as you stand tall in your own creative space that you can truly influence the world for good. Trying to do this any other way will be futile. It will not be registered as authentic. It may look good but it will never truly be good. Real good comes from that place within ourselves that is free of all falsehood.

YOUR NATURAL LIFE'S COURSE

There is a natural course for your life. There is a natural path to your life. Allow yourself to be effortlessly guided on this course. There is a path to the dream in your heart and there is a still small inner voice silently inviting you in that direction. When you choose to go against this natural course, you find that you labor with difficulty in the wrong direction. It is only as you become obedient to the sacred call within your heart that you truly become divine. "There is guidance for each of us" as Emerson says but not everyone chooses to listen.

If you want your life's work to show a striking difference from the work of any other, then it is important to keep your authentic nature. The work that you can do cannot be done by anyone else. The more authentic you become, the more you are able to express your natural inborn creativity.

You don't need to be doing work that is considered important by the world. The only true work is the work imprinted on your soul regardless of how it is rated by the world. What you need to do to protect your dream is to be your authentic self.

If your true purpose is to sweep streets, then sweep the streets with all your heart; if your true purpose is to uplift others, then do that with all your heart. By divine assessment, you will be far better off than those who fool themselves with their inflated egos and are being told by the world that they are important. The emptiness these kinds of people feel on the inside is an obvious pointer to the fact that they are not living on purpose. When you become one with your predestined path, you become truly fulfilled. Accept the place the Divine Presence has created for you and choose that space only. This is enough for you for a whole lifetime.

Ralph Waldo Emerson in his essay, *Spiritual Laws* writes, "A few anecdotes, a few traits of character, manners, faces, a few incidents, have an emphasis in your memory out of all proportion to their apparent significance, if you measure them by ordinary standards. They relate to your gift. Let them have their weight, and do not reject them…What your heart thinks great is great. The soul's emphasis is always right." Indeed your heart knows things intuitively that cannot be known intellectually.

If you want to go far, look without; if you want to go deep, look within. When you dig deep, you discover the ultimate paradox – that the shortest distance is the one that takes you the farthest.

MY DREAM IS DIFFERENT FROM YOURS

There are those whose paths will differ remarkably from yours not because they are not being their authentic selves but because their callings are different. This is where non-judging comes actively into play. They are what they are, you are what you are. There is no need to compare yourself to anyone. You cannot please everyone and even if you try, everyone will not be pleased with you. Give up this futile quest and let yourself live the true life you were made for.

It is only as you communicate your true self that your life truly touches the heart of others. Hearts know hearts and will resonate with all that is genuine and true. There is greatness within everyone but not everyone will harness the greatness within. The truth of your being is what will set you free. It is this truth that will also make you great. The same power that resided in the great men and women of the past also resides in you. What they have done, you can do; where they have gone, you can go; what they became, you can become if only you will be truly aligned with your real self.

HINDRANCES TO CREATIVITY

What are some of the problems we encounter as humans when we try to protect our dreams and in what ways can we safeguard or preserve them?

1) **EDUCATION:** The style of education in many parts of the world, especially in many third world countries is outdated. Very few schools encourage the creativity in a child. Most teachers follow a rigid syllabus oblivious to the fact that every single student is cut from a different cloth. The real role of a teacher is not so much to impart knowledge as to create the enabling environment for students to creatively express themselves.

It is important to facilitate a child's creative potential. The Montessori schools are the closest ones I know to a structure that supports a child's inborn creativity. Teachers should be taught to nurture the creative interests of their students.

Many teachers have a fixed or rigid idea of what a student should be capable of. When a student does something extraordinary that deserves commendation and encouragement, they ignore it and in so doing, fit that student into their box of stereotype and unbelief. This greatly hampers creativity.

There are many teachers who are very good in conveying knowledge but poor when it comes to inciting creativity in their students. There is no telling how far a teacher's influence on a child can go. Many great men and women point to a time in their past when a teacher's encouraging words was the spark they needed to take them past a period of disillusionment.

Sir Ken Robinson, the recipient of the Benjamin Franklin award and a world-renowned education and creativity expert gave a talk on changing education paradigms and how what once worked well in society no longer holds true in a world that is vastly changing and transforming itself.

If more schools would incorporate the creative process into their syllabus, and teach ways to spot and incite creativity in their students, the world would be much farther than it is today and we would have gained much more.

2) **MENTORS:** Growing up, I could see how scarce true mentors were and I am sure a lot of people can relate to this too. A mentor is a leader, but not just a conventional leader. A true mentor inspires

others to be the best they can be by positioning them in an environment that enables their optimum growth. A true mentor does not condemn those who perform poorly at first. True mentors know the importance of giving second chances and understand that gems are usually hidden beneath first failures. True mentors are visionaries. They see the potential in others before others see it in themselves. They are courageous enough to hold on to the good they see even when the voice of the majority says things to the contrary.

True mentors lead by influence, not by force. They lead by example, not just by talk. True mentors are resilient and easily adapt to circumstances. They are able to make the best of everything and are able to create something out of nothing.

True mentors may have a natural propensity towards leading but work at their art everyday. They do not rest on their laurels and they make it a point of duty to keep improving themselves. True mentors do not concern themselves with how much they are known but with how much they have grown. True mentors are admired, respected and followed not because of the position they hold in worldly affairs but because of the place they hold in the people's hearts.

True mentors lead from experience not from intellect. This makes their mentoring process very powerful because they can truly say, "I remember being in this very place. Don't you give up now. The ice will soon melt. It may look like everything is going against you, but if you will just hold on, you will see how wonderful it'll all turn out."

True mentors don't want you becoming like them, they want you becoming like you – the best version of yourself. They do not want you to fill their shoes, they want you to fill your own shoes and shine in your own essence.

Unfortunately, what exists in many third world countries is not this. You find lecturers still using the same notes they used to teach their sophomore class twenty years ago with no adjustments to them whatsoever. They see no need to improve themselves any further and like all things that stop growing, their souls begin to shrivel.

In a place where many people aren't growing in the best way they can, it is much harder for you to protect your dream, especially when your dream is contrary to what is conventional. You will certainly want to have a mentor who has been in your shoes, experienced what you are experiencing and has overcome the obstacles that you face. In this present generation, it is not difficult to see why true mentors are rare.

That said, everyone is a mentor. Everyone influences another person in some way. Everyone's action directly or indirectly affects the lives of countless others. Parents are mentors to their children, siblings are mentors to one another. Bosses are mentors to their employees. Employees are mentors to one another. A cleaner can be a mentor to a gateman.

Mentors do not necessarily have to be older than you are; they just have to have had more experience than you have and there will always be someone who has more experience than you in some particular field. What matters more is not the physical age but the age of maturity.

3) **SOCIETY:** Society plays a key role in supporting or discouraging the dreams of individuals. The intricacy of the problems that plaque countries like Nigeria are so complex that one does not even know where to start from. Organized crime, mismanagement and corruption many times go unpunished. The level of unemployment skyrockets daily. Basic needs of food, clothing and shelter aren't being met and so many people's dreams are dreams of what to eat, what to wear and where to live, not dreams of how best to contribute to the society or give from the best of themselves.

It takes an enormous amount of courage to follow your dream when there are strong forces working night and day to keep you in stagnation or regression. It is very easy to become discouraged and to assume that nothing can be done but this is a false assumption.

A nation gets better as the individuals that make up the nation get better. Primarily it is important to focus on what you can do, because that is your full time job, and when you are truly engaged in your job, you will have no time to dabble into the affairs of other people.

The level of stability in a country goes a long way in supporting or discouraging the dreams of its citizens. A country that is at war or plagued with terrorism and insecurity makes it difficult to encourage the flowering of creativity.

4) **YOURSELF:** The points expatiated above are important and largely determine how fast and how far you pursue your dreams, but none is as important as your ability to overcome the resistance within yourself. Examples abound of individuals who have accomplished

masterfully despite the limitations that surround them because they were able to overcome the limitations that existed within them.

Goethe said, "Until one is committed, there is a hesitancy, the chance to draw back, but the moment one definitely commits oneself, then Providence moves too. All sorts of things occur to help one that would never otherwise have occurred. A whole stream of events issues from the decision, raising in one's favour all manner of unforeseen incidents and meetings and material assistance, which no man could have dreamed would have come his way. Whatever you can do, or dream you can do, begin it. Boldness has genius, power, and magic in it. Begin it now."

When you make a decision to be true to yourself and follow your dream, you are no longer a dabbler, you are a fully committed person and no excuses will do. You will go any length to overcome the resistance that exists on your creative path.

A lot of people are not willing to make this decision because they think it will be too difficult to follow through. They prefer to be complacent and remain in their comfort zone but you see, if you are not constantly challenging and pushing yourself, you lose your natural edge and begin to depreciate. Anything you try that is wholly new will feel uncomfortable at first. It is by following through and making the decision to do it over and over again, that the uncomfortable gradually becomes comfortable and that mountain of impossibility becomes a mole hill of ordered sweetness.

The urge for the status quo has been the cause of many people's withered dreams. After a while, what was once a bright beam sitting elegantly on the pedestal of their heart becomes a flickering bulb about to be snuffed out. They lose the joy of life because the joy of life is contained in doing the work they are made for. Time passes and they wonder how they let precious time fritter away.

Overcoming the resistance within yourself requires a professional mind set. You've got to make the decision not to take success or failure personally. You've got to make the decision to show up when it is time to do your work whether you feel like it or not. You've got to keep on keeping on with the awareness that the more you practice, the stronger your resolve becomes and the better equipped you become to carry out your God-given objectives. Until you reach this place, you will never truly be able to overcome the resistance in the world.

Change is inevitable. It is the only thing that is a constant. It does not yield to your pleading or resisting. It happens in spite of it all. Instead of letting yourself be dragged by life, why not become the person who is a friend of life and not its foe? Instead of resisting the natural course of your life, why not submit yourself, so that life can support you?

It is easy to fill your life with secondary activities. It is easy to get involved in a lot of things that seem important, but really aren't. What you need when dealing with yourself is brutal honesty. The dreams that are meant to lift you up don't put pressure on you. They don't seem urgent, and that is why many people don't do them. Yet, they are the most important work you can ever engage in. To achieve what you are made for, you've got to be proactive. If you just let life roll by, you will be overwhelmed by activities that urgently seek your attention but are not necessarily important or activities that aren't even important at all. You will not be able to achieve your highest potential. You are the one, more than anything else, responsible for making your dreams come true and if you will put in the necessary effort and commitment, you will invariably turn the wheels of life in your favour.

HOW TO PROTECT YOUR DREAM

1) **DON'T LISTEN TO THE OPINIONS OF OTHERS:** The quickest way to kill your dream is to take what people say to you as gospel truth. The quickest way to kill your dream is to try to please everybody. Only you know the dream in your heart and people, though well-meaning, cannot truly tell you your purpose for existing or why you are in the place you are in this time in human history. Don't be naïve - everyone is not going to like you, no matter what you do. Accept this and free yourself to do the best things you are capable of.

In the 2006 movie, *The Pursuit of Happyness* based on the true story of the life of Chris Gardner, Will Smith (who starred as Chris) tells his son, Jaden Smith (Christopher) to protect his dream powerfully, in a way very few are able to eloquently convey: "Don't ever let somebody tell you that you can't do something. Not even me. You got a dream, you have to protect it. Because when people can't do something themselves, they'll want to tell you that you can't do it. If you want something, go get it. Period."

There are many who would like you to remain where you are. Not because deep down, they feel in their hearts it is the best place for you, but because they have failed to listen to their own hearts and are unable to watch you achieve your own dream right before their very eyes without being pricked by their consciences.

Going around eavesdropping on what people are saying about you is a big time waster. It not only blurs your effectiveness, but also obscures the light that shines through you.

Sir Winston Churchill said, "You will never reach your destination if you stop to throw stones at every dog that barks." How true. You will always know deep down in your heart, if somebody else's criticism is credible. Weigh direct criticisms on your heart's scale. Take those that deserve to stand and use them to build an armour around yourself. Cast those that don't away like paper darts because they can't do you any real harm.

2) **GIVE YOURSELF ENOUGH GOOD REASONS:** Your reasons for waking up by 4 am everyday must be stronger than your reasons for staying back in bed. Your reasons for doing a 45-minute work-out everyday must be stronger than your reasons for letting it slip by. Your reasons for following and achieving the dreams of your heart, must be stronger than your reasons for not doing so. Everything you do must be backed up by good enough reasons.

Sit down and write down your goals. Write down 5 reasons why it is absolutely important to achieve them and let those reasons drive you on to achieve more than you thought possible. Your determination and dedication will edge its way through any obstacle, no matter what it may be.

Some of the common reasons people give for achieving their dreams are:

i) I won't be here forever. Let me do what needs to be done while I still have the strength.

ii) Time waits for no one. Days quickly turn into weeks and weeks quickly turn into months and months quickly turn into years. Life fades away quicker than I imagine.

iii) My children deserve the very best and I am willing to put in my very best to make them experience that.

iv) My parents labored long and hard to give me a good education. I am not willing to let that go unrewarded.

v) I only live life once and so I must be true to myself in this life.

3) **BE COGNIZANT OF YOUR ASSOCIATIONS:** I cannot overemphasize this point. We are always affected by those we habitually associate ourselves with. Don't let yourself be deceived. The more time you spend with someone, the more their character rubs off on you. If you stay around losers – people who have no idea what they intend to do with their lives, you will eventually begin to think like them. Benjamin Franklin rightly quipped, "Do not squander time, for that is the stuff life is made out of". If you associate with people who are always working to surpass their former

selves, who are ever ready to get up when they fail and persist no matter the resistance, they will begin to influence you. You too will begin to believe that you can achieve the dream that has been placed in your heart from the beginning of the world. So watch your associations closely. They matter a lot.

Ask yourself these questions Jim Rohn poses:

i) Who am I around?

ii) What are they doing to me? What have they got me thinking? What have they got me saying? What have they got me believing?

iii) Is that OK?

These are personal reflective questions which should be honestly answered by you. And when you find those answers, take swift steps to let those who are not of the same truth as you fall away while drawing closer to those who uplift and inspire you.

4) **BE TRUE TO YOURSELF:** Jeremiah, one of the prophets of the Old testament, said "The heart is deceitful above all things and it is exceedingly corrupt. Who can understand it?" Self-delusion is the easiest form of delusion. The mind is very smart and will easily cook up stories as to why you need to wait one more day or one more week or one more month before beginning the work which you were made for. If you give ear to this, you begin to live a lie.

Be true to yourself. Refuse to let what others have or haven't done prevent you from achieving what you are capable of. Let the outcome of your work be proof to yourself and to others of the magnificence that resides within you.

5) **DISCIPLINE YOURSELF:** In the end, it all boils down to the work you have to do. Nothing can replace that. No amount of dreaming or believing will by itself bring your dreams to pass. You've got to put action to it. You will be surprised at what you can achieve when you consistently dedicate a little amount of time everyday to caring for your dreams.

Everything magnificent in the world today started out as a dream in somebody's mind and would have remained a dream if they only stopped at that. When you get to the place where you no longer just dream dreams, but begin to live them, your life takes on a special power of its own.

Don't let yourself be deceived. God will not do the work we can do for ourselves, just as we cannot do the work that God alone can do. Let your most effective prayer be your action because nothing else can take its place.

REFERENCES
Chapter One
1. Do It Anyway: The Handbook for Finding Personal Meaning and Deep Happiness in a Crazy World by Kent M. Keith
2. Ralph Waldo Emerson: His Life, Writings, and Philosophy by George Willis Cooke
3. Empower the Leader in You! By Joan F. Marques
4. Think Twice: You Can Be Creative by Jasmine Renner
5. The Element: How Finding Your Passion Changes Everything by Ken Robinson, Lou Aronica
6. On Becoming a Leader by Warren Bennis
7. Reprogram Your Mind for Success and Happiness by Cleophus Jackson
8. The Cambridge Companion to Mark Twain edited by Forrest G. Robinson
9. Believe You Can – The Power of a Positive Attitude by John Mason
10. The Wisdom of the Great by Sam Majdi
11. Be What You Want to Be: Heal Yourself by Darlene Nelson
12. Twelve Things You Were Not Taught in School About Creative Thinking by Michael Michalko
13. Why Don't Students Like School? By Daniel T. Willingham

Chapter Two
1. A Return to Love: Reflections on the Principles of A Course in Miracles by Marianne Williamson
2. A Course in Miracles edited by Helen Schucman and William T. Thetford
3. Bible Exposition Commentary: Old Testament, the Prophets by Warren W. Wiersbe
4. Late Bloomer – Wikipedia.org
5. The Works of William Shakespeare, Volume 6 by William Shakespeare
6. Heavenly Wisdom: Talent, Imagination, Creativity and Wisdom by Dragan P. Bogunovic
7. The Invitation by Oriah Mountain Dreamer
8. The Works of Mr. William Shakespeare: In Eight Volumes By William Shakespeare
9. Quotes by Horace by QuotationsBook.com

Chapter Three
1. Tantra: The Supreme Understanding by Osho
2. Prov. 16:18
3. Five Levels of Attachment: Toltec Wisdom for the Modern World by Don Miguel Ruiz, Jr.

4. The Utne Reader, Issue 91
5. Secrets of the Heart: Finding the Key to a Joyous Life by Richard W. Dortch
6. The Pocket Rumi by Mevlana Jalaluddin Rumi
7. 1 Timothy 6:6
8. Relationships – True Love and the Transcendence of Duality by Kim Eng (with Eckhart Tolle)
9. The Complete 101 Collection: What Every Leader Needs to Know by John C. Maxwell
10. Relationships 101 by John C. Maxwell
11. A New Earth: Awakening to Your Life's Purpose by Eckhart Tolle
12. Luke 23:24

Chapter Four
1. Robert Frost: The Ethics of Ambiguity by John H. Timmerman
2. Complete Tom Sawyer by Mark Twain
3. A treasury of Kahlil Gibran by Kahlil Gibran
4. The Collected Works of Ralph Waldo Emerson Volume 2 edited by Alfred Riggs Ferguson
5. Telling It Like It Is: A book of quotations by Paul Bowden
6. Walden by Henry David Thoreau
7. Lao-tzu and the Tao te Ching: Studies in Ethics, Law, and the Human Ideal edited by Livia Kohn and Michael LaFargue
8. God Said by Benjamin Paul Ciaccio II
9. Wit and wisdom of Gandhi by Mahatma Gandhi
10. Life's Greatest Lessons: 20 Things That Matter by Hal Urban

Chapter Five
1. The Complete Works of William Shakespeare by William Shakespeare
2. The Spiritual Teachings of Ralph Waldo Emerson by Richard G. Geldard
3. Quotes about Will and Will Power by QuotationsBooks.com
4. Essays and Poems by Ralph Waldo Emerson
5. A Course in Miracles edited by Helen Schucman and William T. Thetford
6. Essays by Ralph Waldo Emerson
7. God's Wisdom for Your Life by Tina Krause

Chapter Six
1. Your Best Life Now: 7 Steps to Living at Your Full Potential by Joel Osteen
2. Essays by Ralph Waldo Emerson
3. Excuses Begone!: How to Change Lifelong Self-defeating Thinking Habits by Wayne W. Dyer
4. The Lenzy Kelley Book of Sayings by Bubba

5. Veronica Decides to Die by Paulo Coelho
6. Blaise Pascal: Reasons of the Heart by Marvin Richard O'Connell
7. Civil Disobedience by Henry David Thoreau
8. The Creative Compass: Writing Your Way from Inspiration to Publication by Dan Millman and Sierra Prasada
9. Prov. 4:23, Matt. 13:12
10. A Better Way to Live by Og Mandino
11. As a Man Thinketh by James A. Allen
12. The Olympic Odyssey: Rekindling the True Spirit of the Great Games by Phil Cousineau

Chapter Seven
1. The Book of Life by Robert Collier
2. Being the Christ of Today: 7 Ways to Transform Your life and Heal the World by Michael Merritt
3. The Four Agreements: A Practical Guide to Personal Freedom by Don Miguel Ruiz
4. What Really Matters: 7 Lessons for Living from the Stories of the Dying by Karen M. Wyatt
5. Siddhartha, Demian, and Other Writings by Hermann Hesse
6. Question Your Thinking, Change the World by Byron Katie
7. The Road Less Traveled: A New Psychology of Love, Traditional Values and Spiritual Growth by M. Scott Peck, M.D.
8. Now is the Time by Jim McMullan
9. Stepping Stones by Bryan Britton
10. Uprising (Album) by Bob Marley and the Wailers: Redemption Song
11. Rediscover the Power of Your Identity: Unlocking Your Potential for Lasting Excellency by Johnstone Kayandabila
12. Journal of Abnormal Psychology 2000, Vol 109, No. 1, 150-155, University of Oxford's Center for Suicide Research.

Chapter Eight
1. Melody Beattie 4 Title Bundle: Codependent No More and Others by Melody Beattie
2. Job 1:21
3. Two Strangers – One Soul by Bob Norton
4. Ecc. 9:4
5. Turning Passions into Profits: Three Steps to Wealth and Power by Christopher Howard
6. See You at the Top by Zig Ziglar
7. Mentoring 101: What Every leader Needs to Know by John Maxwell

Chapter Nine
1. Matt. 7:1-2

2. Mohandas K. Gandhi: Thoughts, Words, Deeds by Ramnarine Sahadeo
3. The Collected Works of Ralph Waldo Emerson Volume 2 edited by Alfred Riggs Ferguson
4. Never Stop Laughing! By William Goodman
5. Uprising (Album) by Bob Marley and the Wailers: Redemption Song
6. The Conduct of Life by Ralph Waldo Emerson
7. Love Life by Cinique Scott
8. Luke 23:24
9. The Daily Motivator (http://greatday.com) by Ralph S. Marston, Jr.
10. 101 Selected Sayings of Buddha by Irfan Alli
11. Spiritual Gems from Mother Teresa by Gwen Costello
12. The Power of Intention: Learning to Co-Create Your World Your Way by Wayne W. Dyer
13. A Course in Miracles edited by Helen Schucman and William T. Thetford
14. Fat Into the Fire by David P. Morrow

Chapter Ten
1. Mental Hygiene: Essays on Writers and Writing by Ray Robertson
2. Ralph Waldo Emerson: His Life, Writings, and Philosophy by George Willis Cooke
3. Wisdom for the Soul: Five Milennia of Prescriptions for Spiritual Healing edited by Larry Chang
4. Rom 12:18
5. The Steps Of A Good Man by DivineCrossingsx, Incorporated
6. Essays by Ralph Waldo Emerson
7. The sutra of 42 sections
8. The Creativity Post: Einstein's Gift for Fantasy by Michael Michalko
9. Visions and Leadership in Sustainable Development by Chris Maser
10. Golf is the Teacher, Life is the Lesson by Daniel Stewart Acuff Ph.D
11. Winston S. Churchill: His Complete Speeches, 1897-1963: 1922-1928

ABOUT THE AUTHOR

Babatunde Kolawole is a medical doctor based in Abuja, Nigeria, whose calling is to influence and inspire people to be their best selves through the power of spoken and written words. His heart-felt messages cut across people of all ages, races, creeds and nationalities.

Printed in Dunstable, United Kingdom